GOLDEN
TONES

Walter Green

Let him who knows his instrument play it.

—Spanish Proverb

"No composer has ever understood the qualities of individual instruments as did Mozart ... with the bassoon, it is like a Sea-god speaking."—Sacheverell Sitwell

"The bassoon is one of my favorite instruments. It has the medieval aroma, like the days when everything used to sound like that. Some people crave baseball ... I find this unfathomable, but I can easily understand why a person could get excited about playing the bassoon."—Frank Zappa

"I was often asked why I chose to play the bassoon. The answer is simple and might be the same for many other bassoonists: in my youth, students for this instrument were very scarce so when I wanted to enter the Vienna Conservatory the Dean of this prominent Academie offered me every course free of all tuition if only I would take up the bassoon. The student orchestra that year did not have even one, so the instrument was really in demand."

—Hugo Burghauser

GOLDEN
TONES

by
WALTER GREEN

MEMOIRS OF A MUSICIAN'S LIFE

as told to

BRUCE LEVENE

Pacific Transcriptions
Mendocino, California

Published by Pacific Transcriptions
P.O. Box 526   Mendocino, California   95460
(707) 937-4801   pactrans@mcn.org

ISBN Number 0-933391-24-2
Library of Congress Control Number: 2003116368

Front cover painting by Bruce Wolfe
Cover design by Gopa and Ted2
Back cover photograph by Stephen Gillette

On Hearing a Symphony of Beethoven
—from **The Buck in the Snow and Other Poems**
© 1928 by Edna St. Vincent Millay

First Edition

Contents

Acknowledgements

My deep gratitude to my friend and editor, Bruce Levene, for working so hard on this project, for helping me to bring forth my life stories through his keen questioning, and for his knowledge and love of classical music.

To Joseph Handlon who encouraged me to write this book and whose friendship is so very much appreciated.

My heartfelt gratitude to my children, Nancy Allouche, David Green, and Peter Green, who have given me constant encouragement to tell this tale.

My family tree changed when I married Polly, and her daughters, Jennifer, Sari, Katie and Sioban, continue to bring grace and beauty to my life

Bruce Wolfe has been a friend for many years and his painting of me, completed some time ago, now graces the cover of this book.

Thank you to Rabbi Margaret Holub for her continual spiritual guidance and love.

My gratitude to Henrietta Bensussen and Elinor Pravda for their editorial suggestions, and to Marge Smith, who transcribed the interviews.

Finally, to my wife, Polly, whose companionship, love and extraordinary insights made it possible for me to persevere and bring forth **Golden Tones**.

Foreword

I t is always amazing to me how a decision to make a simple phone call can result in anything so profound as a close friendship lasting over many years. But this was the end result of my phoning Walter Green back in the early '60's to ask if he would give me bassoon lessons. Oh, true, I had played other musical instruments before, starting out on the violin when I was nine years old. As a matter of fact, I had played oboe and English horn professionally for several years beginning when I was eighteen. I had, indeed, been fortunate enough to have played under such famous conductors as Beecham, Monteux, Stravinsky, and Dorati. But increasingly I had suffered from performance anxiety, and had finally given up playing professionally some five years after I had begun.

By then in the '60's when I first called Walter, I had a Ph. D. in psychology, was in my early 40's, and was an Associate Professor of Psychiatry at the Stanford Medical School. I had developed a hankering to play the bassoon just for fun. I had tried to pick it up on my own, but it soon became obvious that I needed lessons, not only in bassoon playing per se, but in reed making. So I was disappointed when Walter Green, with whom I had been most impressed when I had heard him play with the San Francisco Symphony and with the San Francisco Opera, did not return my phone call right away.

When he finally did call back, we set up an appointment to see each other at his home in the Sunset District in San Francisco. The house was located on an elliptically-shaped street that was once the site of a famous old San Francisco race track. I showed up for my first lesson with my very poor quality rental bassoon, a reed case with a couple of commercial reeds that I had hacked away at, not knowing what I was doing (I had, of course, previously learned to make my own oboe reeds) and one plastic bassoon reed that I had tried out. It soon became obvious that if I were serious about learning to play the bassoon—even just for my own pleasure—that I would have to get a somewhat decent instrument. Walter could arrange for that; which he promptly did. He also provided me with an excellent reed, freshly made on the spot. I already possessed a standard exercise book for the bassoon, so we were on our way. Of course, I had to unlearn a lot of old oboe habits, about how to hold the reed in my mouth—mostly how to relax the overly tight typical oboe embouchure.

To my delight, I quickly could see that Walter was quite psychologically sophisticated. No doubt that was due, in part, to the fact that his elder brother was a practicing psychiatrist in the Detroit area, and that Walter's wife, Charlotte, was a social worker. I learned, too, that Walter also experienced the discomforts of performance anxiety himself, so that he was more than a little sympathetic with what I had experienced playing professionally.

After a few years, I moved away to take a faculty position in Cleveland, Ohio and became increasingly involved in Gestalt Psychology and Therapy. When Walter asked me for a therapy recommendation, I suggested that he find a Gestalt therapist in the Bay Area, which he did. As an indication of Walter's creativity, I was delighted to learn subsequently that he had successfully applied some of the basic principles of Gestalt Psychology in his music teaching. Other music teachers would do well to emulate this innovative approach.

During my brief time as a professional musician, I had encountered many competent musicians who, perhaps, almost matched Walter's general caliber of excellence in performance, but who were merely superior mechanics, whose overall view of life was extremely parochial at best and narrowly prejudiced and distorted at worst. This was both a puzzlement and a terrible disappointment to me: "How can you play the world's great masterpieces and yet have such little minds?" I used to wonder. As you will soon see from this book about his life, Walter has been able to approach both his art and his life from a number of broad perspectives. In addition to the perspective which his psychological sophistication has given him, here are some other of Walter's special qualities that come easily to mind.

First is his cultural heritage. Although you will read about Walter coming to this country to escape from Hitler, I can also vividly recall how warmly he spoke of the pleasure he got from reading Rilke's poetry in the original German. Further, Walter's relatively recent attempts to relocate his family roots in Germany have been matched by his enthusiastic interest in delving into his religious roots in the last few years — both of which activities you will find sensitively captured in his own words.

Next, one of Walter's characteristics that I have personally enjoyed the most over the years is his delicious sense of humor. It can be soft and delicate or as loud and bawdy as one would want; but I have never heard it be used directly in a teasing, mean, or put-down fashion. Musicians are notorious practical jokesters — as when Sir Thomas Beecham was "arrested" during a morning Hollywood Bowl rehearsal for having played the National Anthem too fast at a performance the night before. Walter and I have had many a laugh together sharing stories of such famous (and infamous) practical jokes. We have also had lots of laughs over the foibles of the various conductors we have known. In addition, Walter's *sotto voce* side comments during overly-long, tedious rehearsals have helped pass the time for more than one worn out crew of fellow players.

From our very first encounter, I have always been impressed with Walter's sensitivity in dealing with others. I have seen this in the way he interacts with friends, with the way he conducts rehearsals, and with the way he deals with his three grown children, Nancy, David, and Peter. Walter's relationship with his wife, Polly, is lovely to see in their mutual caring, sensitivity and awareness.

As you will discover, Walter's chronicle of his life is a poignant journey during an important time in our contemporary history. You will observe that it has been a journey full of joys and sorrows, a journey full of near tragedies (as when his house literally blew up) and real tragedies (the untimely death of Charlotte), yet of triumphs. I feel honored to have shared a part of that journey.

—*Joseph H. Handlon, Ph.D.*
Santa Barbara, California
July, 2003

Preface

I usually go to the Mendocino Post Office about 12:30. One day in April, 2003 I picked up my mail late in the afternoon. Twenty minutes earlier and you might not be reading this preface, because I would not have encountered Gordon Black, philosopher and music lover. I've known Gordon for many years and he's a good acquaintance. Three or four times a year we meet and chat for a few minutes. Gordon told me that his friend, Walter Green, was working on a book and needed editorial advice. I agreed to phone him.

Walter Green had lived here for 20 years and I came to the Coast 35 years ago, but we had never met. I knew of him, of course, that he had been instrumental in founding the Mendocino Music Festival and that he played recordings of classical music on the radio every Friday morning. I would listen to his *The Wonderous World of Music* on KZYX, appreciate his musical commentaries, and usually liked the recordings he played. Until that time, however, my only relationship with Walter Green was that of a radio listener.

A few weeks later I phoned Walter. Well, he didn't just want editorial help—he wanted his life story recorded, then transcribed and edited into a completed book. I was hesitant about undertaking a new project, but no doubt Walter had a good story to tell, so we decided to discuss his book.

I have met many musical performers and know they are different than I am. They perform and they play music, two elements that divide them from those who don't. It is difficult for non-musical people to personally get close to musicians. Undoubtedly it also works the other way. For over 60 years Walter Green was a professional musician. His life and orchestral music were inseparable and virtually all his friends were musicians. I, on the other hand, haven't touched an instrument since I played trombone in high school band more than a half century ago. Walter had never met a certifiable record collector or known anyone who knew as much about music—at least recorded music—as I do, who wasn't either a musician or a dedicated concertgoer. My interests have always been the sounds and the intellectual thoughts that created those sounds; Walter's interest was producing the sounds themselves.

We agreed to have one hour recording sessions. I thought that 15 interviews should be adequate for Walter to relate his life story. Little did I know that it would take 24 interviews and a year's work. But before beginning, we had to establish a rapport. A definite reserve existed on Walter's part. How could there not be? He must have thought, "Who is this stranger who arrogantly says he knows so much about music—but also states that he can't read a note? He comes into my house, sits me down before a microphone and begins to ask personal questions." If you are introspective and played Principal Bassoon in world-class orchestras for 34 years, the experience would be unnerving.

The first interview was strained; we were both feeling our way. Walter didn't quite understand that in the oral history process it is necessary to relate events somewhat chronologically. He mentioned that the first orchestra he played in during the 1950s was the Indianapolis Symphony. "Was Fabien Sevitsky the conductor then?" I asked. Surprised that anyone would know such an obscure fact, Walter almost fell out of his chair. But at that moment he knew that I might be a worthy listener, and that we were peers in our relationship. We clicked!

Walter's life story is important. Not only did he become a good musician, he was one of the best bassoonists in the history of music. No small accomplishment, considering the social and economic adversities, beginning with his family's escape from Hitler's Germany, that plagued his early years. Throughout his long life he maintained a dedication to play the bassoon as well as it can be played, in a graceful quest for both ultimate performance and the greatest musical appreciation.

Autobiographical works are usually produced with the hope that one's descendants might have a better understanding, if not love, of the writer. This book is also a gift to Walter's (and my) ancestors.

—*Bruce Levene*
Mendocino
April, 2004

Chapter 1
Germany
1926 — 1938

My love of music came to me from my blessed parents and undoubtedly from their parents also. My father loved to play violin in community orchestras. I used to go to rehearsals with him when I was three years old. Whenever I visited my grandparents Hirsch when I was a little boy, it was usually on a Saturday night, and we slept over. My grandfather would wake me up at six o'clock Sunday morning, put me tenderly on his lap in the living room, turn on the radio, and we'd share listening to the music that came from the *Thomaskirche*, one of Johann Sebastian Bach's churches in Leipzig. I learned a lot about Bach when I was four years old and I learned a lot about loving grandpas. It's something that I remember wistfully, contrasting with the awful way that my grandparents died in the concentration camp. My grandfather loved Bach. I guess the music of Johann Sebastian Bach and his sons is forever. Grandfather Hirsch, who was a cantor for some years, had a lovely voice. My Jewish faith was very deeply grounded and, combined with music, that faith gave me what was necessary to live my life in a spiritual context. And the spiritual part of me is tied to music and playing with symphony orchestras. Thus, I was "tunnel-visioned" as to the direction of my life.

I was born August 11, 1926 in Iserlohn, a small town near Essen in northwest Germany, not far from Belgium.

Mendener String Orchestra, 1929
Paul Eichengrün, back row, sixth from right

That day was also the Constitution Day of the Weimar Republic. According to my father, at the moment of my birth a brass band came down the street and played the German national anthem, *Deutschland über Alles*. That was the Constitution Day for Walter Green.

My father was named Paul Eichengrün. He was descended from a long line of Eichengrüns and had many relatives. A distant cousin, Ludwig Eichengrün, saw the German tragedy developing and wrote a history of the Eichengrün clan in Westphalia. This document was sent to Israel in 1944 and remained there until Israel became a nation in 1948. I received a copy of it several years after the end of World War II.

Because certain words used in the document do not belong to the German language, it is surmised that the origin of the clan must have been Sephardic, members of that large group of Jews who were exiled from Spain, beginning on the very day in 1492 when Columbus sailed for the New

2

World. Before their move into Germany, the Eichengrün family (the name Eichengrün means oak green) had settled in Alsace, so they were thought to have been Alsatian. Some migrated to Belgium. I have a German Haggadah that belonged to an Eichengrün cousin; it has a stamp from Belgium. My cousin in Israel, Josef Zur, constructed a fantastic family tree that shows part of the Eichengrün family moved first to a little German town called Beringhausen. The earliest known Eichengrün there was Moyses Simon Eichengrün, who was born in 1761. The Jews must have been in Beringhausen for many years because they had the protection of the Archbishop of Cologne. Everyone else in the diocese screwed them royally as no one other than the Archbishop, who was very protective of the Jewish people in that part of Germany, cared for them.

In 1914, at the beginning of the First World War, my father enlisted in the German Army. He joined the infantry and spent four years in the trenches, two years on the Russian front and two years on the Western front. He was wounded and remained a private for all four years of service, because Jews did not easily get advancement in rank. Dad was a confirmed pacifist by the end of his tour of duty. He was discharged in 1918 and went into business with his Uncle

Paul Eichengrün 1917

3

Sigmund. They founded the firm of S&P Eichengrün, a wholesale business that sold tailor notions: needles, thread, and fabric. My father started out as a salesman. The business had a chauffeur. I am talking about the 1920s and having a chauffeur did not mean he was wealthy, only that Uncle Sigmund was not a good driver and they needed someone to chauffeur them around. Dad and Uncle Sigmund prided themselves on having a good business. But in 1926, because of political and economic conditions, inflation came to Germany and when the Deutsche Mark became worthless their business was wiped out.

My mother's maiden name was Paula Hirsch. During the First World War she went to business school in Kassel and worked at becoming an accountant. She told me that they ate mostly turnips during the War. Her family were middle class people and had to struggle in order to make it.

The first four years of my life our family lived in Menden. My maternal grandparents helped my father get a job there

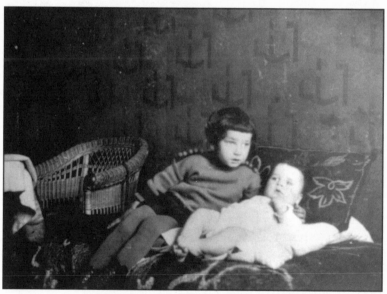

Ralph Eichengrün, Walter Eichengrün 1926

as a general agent for an insurance company. Then we moved to Lippstadt, a town of perhaps 12,000 inhabitants, where my older brother Ralph and I started our schooling.

When Hitler came to power in Germany in 1933, people organized torchlight parades. Even a little town like Lippstadt had a torchlight parade. The *SA*, Hitler's brown-shirted thugs, organized things in a most expeditious manner. I went to school

Walter Eichengrün, Ralph Eichengrün 1929

the next day and the Army brought in pots of soup in large kettles. Those big containers were drawn by Army horses and inside was hot soup for kids who were hungry and for those kids who didn't have any food at home. You could tell parents were thinking to themselves, "Gee, he is feeding our kids, he must be all right." The Third Reich was the people's comfort. These kinds of activities were enough to swing the whole country towards the Nazis. The German Army did a good deed for the children of their land and got the whole town to support the transfer of power. The constitution of the Weimar Republic (which came into existence after World War I), was valuable as a document, but forcing this ideal onto the German people was impossible if they were hungry—because no matter how democracy is forced onto people they don't necessarily know how to live with it, or without it.

Conditions changed rapidly after Hitler gained power. My parents took us to the voting poll and assured us this would be the last free election in Germany, especially with *SA* goons hanging over our shoulders. In 1933 I was seven years old, and had little knowledge of the Germany of years past. After Hitler became chancellor, life became very difficult for my parents. My grandparents and an uncle helped us financially. Grandfather Hirsch had a small clothing store. Dad still had his insurance business, but one had to be careful because people were disappearing right and left. Some of our best friends ended up in concentration camps.

I started school when I was six years old. There were about ten Jewish boys in the school. A few days following Hitler's rise to power, school teachers started telling us the story about Richard Wagner and his mythological hero, Sigfried, who according to the Nazi mythology was killed by the Jews. Some Jews climbed up a hill where Sigfried lay sleeping and threw heavy stones at him. The stones hit him in the back at the one spot where he wasn't covered by the blood of the Dragon. It really took a lot of imagination to draw the Jewish children into this myth. Even Wagner didn't express that in his operas. Imagine what it felt like for those of us who were Jewish sitting in the classroom listening to this gigantic lie. For me, it was terrifying.

After school I went to visit my grandparents and the Nazis were busy painting the store windows black, with the words "*Jude*! Don't buy here," in large letters on the store building. The Nazi goons would come and sing in front of our apartment and they sang about dirty Jews and filthy Jews and how the Jews had ruined their precious country.

Once I came from Hebrew school and was chased down the street by an *SS* man. He was actually in the Gestapo because he had a Death's Head insignia on his cap. I raced all the way to my grandmother's house, who lived the closest. Everybody in that small town of Lippstadt knew everyone else and no one had an excuse for not knowing about this ugliness.

I remember when we spent four weeks in the little town of Nideggen, which was located south of the River Rhine. We were eating our dessert and a group of Nazis came and started singing these hideous songs and breaking every window in the *pension*. We were filled with anxiety and fear. We just had to take what came and make the best of a very fearful situation.

We as a family were hard hit by little ailments, which showed the strain we were under. Mom had some kind of recurring stomach ulcer. My own anxiety was so intense that I became anemic, which lasted until 1938, even though it was treated immediately. Thank goodness there was a Jewish Doctor Rath in our town to help take care of us. Dr. Rath left Lippstadt in 1938 and ended his years in Watertown, New York.

My brother Ralph was three-and-a-half-years older than me. He and I kept each other company when no other child would play with us because of our Jewish heritage.

Ralph hated fish. He would sit gnawing at his noonday meal with his fish, afraid of dying because he might swallow a fish bone. I mention this only because all this tension made us anxious beyond belief and we didn't even know it.

The oppression of the Jews in our town started in early 1933, shortly after Hitler took power. A man named Paul Mossbach made a joke about Hitler while in the Post Office. He disappeared and was never seen again.

The anxiety that comes with this kind of fear has lasted my whole life. I was a performing musician in major orchestras for more than 50 years and have never gotten over taking tranquilizers. Anxiety brings with it all kinds of misery and I have experienced a lot of that. Of course, my parents were the hardest hit, as those were very difficult times in which to nurture their family.

I have often asked myself how I maintained hope as a child at such a young age. My father often invited our gym teacher, Herr Witte, to our Sabbath meal. People were grateful to be blessed by the Jewish doctrine of sharing food on the Sabbath day. Amazingly, the teacher Witte became the worst Nazi of all the people in Lippstadt. When we were all lined up in the schoolyard, the teacher threw a medicine ball at my head and it took a few days for it to heal. My father went to the principal and asked him why it was that the gym teacher had thrown a medicine ball right on my nose. The principal said, "Herr Eichengrün, there is nothing I can do. I am sorry."

When we went to the swimming pool, Herr Witte tried to drown me and almost succeeded in his evil work. School became a horrendous anguish for me. This has affected me ever since and learning to swim is the least important thing I can think of. To stay in balance is necessary in one's life, and most assuredly friendship still brings me balance and hope.

One Sunday morning in 1935 we were in the middle of breakfast and the doorbell rang. Dad said, "Walter, open the door and see who that is." I opened the door and there was an *SS* man standing at the entrance. I don't think I have ever been so scared. The *SS* man said, "May I talk with your father." My father came running out and the *SS* man said, "The *Führer* gives you his greeting and a commendation medal for being in the First World War for four years." That was the only time my father received any reward for his German Army service.

My father was a politically active Zionist. His sister joined a Zionist movement in her teens and wanted to leave the country for Palestine. Her parents wouldn't allow it. That was when we, as Zionists, were not considered evil. People like my aunt and uncle and my father and mother were most enthusiastic Zionists—most wonderfully idealistic human beings.

My parents were very liberal. They didn't speak Yiddish, nor did my grandparents. This was probably because they were of Sephardic desecent, not Ashkenazi (eastern European). Smaller communities were very conservative. If you thought about *yiddishkeit* you thought about being either orthodox or conservative. There was only one synagogue in our little town and we had Sunday school on Monday afternoon. I don't know why on Monday afternoon. That's the way it worked out.

In Lippstadt we had friends, the Levys, who owned a toy store. The anti-Semitism became so vicious that they had to close the store. I don't know what happened to them. I suspect they died in Auschwitz. They invited my brother and me to come to their store and pick out whatever toys we wanted. My brother chose a steam engine, the kind that makes its own steam and has a wheel that pushes things around. I chose a record player with a record of a composition by Mozart. I feel really good about that choice because music came first from the very beginning.

Ralph and I played recorders at home with Dad, who played the violin. We'd make up tunes and play many Jewish folk songs. My brother continued to play the flute even after he received his doctorate. My father, brother, and I never performed publicly. I played recorder in my grade-school orchestra and that brought me solace. We were permitted to play with the school orchestra, but only when the teachers allowed us to play. The anti-Semitic teachers made us suffer.

One time my father, brother, and I went to the circus. There were wonderful circuses in Europe. A clown in the middle of the main ring blew into a piece of pipe and, would

Ralph Eichengrün, Paula Eichengrün, Walter Eichengrün 1933

you believe it, out came a bassoon in a parachute. The clown put it in his mouth and began to play. Father didn't know what it was because he had spent his life with string instruments. Of course, I didn't know what it was, nor did I care.

I stayed in Essen for a couple of months with my mother's sister and brother, Aunt Elsa and Uncle Walter. My aunt later became my stepmother after my mother died. I went to an *SA* meeting in downtown Essen. There was a lot of noise going on down the street. I investigated it and found myself immersed in band music and marching *SA* men. The speaker at the meeting was Adolph Hitler and his speech was so powerful that I was cheering as loud as the goons of the Third Reich. This is hard to understand. It was 1936 and the power of Hitler's words enveloped even *me*.

Once my parents realized how devastating the anti-Semitism was in our small town for my brother and me, they sent us to large cities to be unnoticed and to stay unnoticed. My brother was sent to Essen to stay with Aunt Elsa and Uncle Walter. I was placed with my father's sister Marta and her husband and two children, Abraham and Yossi, in Cologne. There was a Jewish school in Cologne known as *Yafne*, which prepared young people for a life in Israel. Later Abraham and Yossi helped to build kibbutzim, one in the Golan Heights and one in the Negev desert. They are our blessed heroes and grand souls and totally devoted to the cause of Israel.

All the things that happened to us were a consequence of the stupidity and insensitivity of people who allowed freedom to slip away. Germany before Hitler was very beautiful: physically beautiful, culturally beautiful, and amazingly musical. How could they have so defaced this beautiful country and its people? Before 1933 Germany was a cultural nation, but after 1933 only one thing mattered, "How can we support the Führer and his ideology?"

In 1933 my parents started thinking about making a move, either to the United States or Palestine. It took five and a half years after applying for a visa, until 1938, for us to be able to leave Germany, which is an amazingly long time. All kinds of things happened during those years. You had to have relatives in the United States to get a visa. You sure did! One of our relatives, *Tante* Mally and her parents, moved to the United States at the beginning of the twentieth century, but then she decided to go back to Germany in 1908. I saw them in Israel after Israel became a nation. *Tante* Mally was always one of my favorite relatives. She was the wife of the man who shared the notions business with my father.

Dad corresponded with distant cousins in the United States. They were all over the place. There was a banker in Texas who was somehow related to us, but when we asked him for help to get a visa he was never heard from again.

There were cousins who did try to help us. One in Nor-wich, Connecticut owned a ranch with seven buildings on it. The American Immigration and Naturalization Service rejected the application because they found out one of the buildings was an outhouse. The cousins all pitched in to get the property values high enough so the INS and Inter-nal Revenue Service would allow their meager values to be acceptable. The American government wanted to be sure that it wouldn't have to support us after we arrived in the United States.

My parents tried everything possible to make this miracle happen and they succeeded in 1938. My father essentially bought the visas, by paying off the American consul and the Gestapo. The American Consul General in Stuttgart examined us and said, "I can let all of you go except Mr. Green." My mother said, "Why not my husband!" The Consul General said, "Because your husband has varicose veins." Mom said "That is not enough to keep someone from emigrating." The Consul General said, "It is very ex-pensive for an American to live here in Stuttgart." My par-ents responded with a lot of money. In 1942 the FBI visited us and wanted to know more about this Consul General. We gave them details and pictures and later learned that the Consul General ended his career in Leavenworth. There is justice in this world after all.

I'm not sure how the people received exit visas from the German government. I know that people came out in all kinds of ways. My cousins in Los Angeles were put on a *kindertransport* (children's transport) and met their parents in Holland. That was before the German army reached Holland during the War. On *Kristallnacht*, my Uncle Ernst was beaten and put into a concentration camp, but some-how he escaped.

My relatives who survived the Holocaust or even the pre-Holocaust were scattered all over the world. I will never see them again, except for my cousins in Israel and two cousins, Greta and Ernie Simon, who escaped just before the war and settled in Pittsburgh, Pennsylvania. In 1939 my cousins Jossi and Abraham went to Palestine and joined a kibbutz. It was hard to enter Palestine then because the British Mandate tried to prevent immigration. My cousins were put on a kindertransport to that beloved country. They entered junior high school in Palestine. One of them went to school with the daughter of the British High Commissioner of Palestine and begged the High Commissioner to allow his family entrance into Palestine. Their parents as well as our joint grandmother, aunt, and uncle were saved. The family entered Palestine the 31st of August 1939.

Everyone survived except for my maternal grandparents. Everyone else left Germany. My grandparents could have received a visa but they said, "You know, we have lived here in Germany all our lives and do not want to leave our homeland." I can really understand that. I'm 76 years old now and if that kind of virulent behavior occurred here and my children told me I could go to Canada or stay in the United States, I would choose the latter. *Opa* and *Oma* stayed because of their love of their homeland. They loved where they were and they had spent their whole life in relative middle class ease. Grandmother and Grandfather Hirsch were deported to Theresienstadt and died there in 1941. Their blessed memory is with us eternally.

I asked my father twenty years ago, "How come, with our Zionist sympathies, we ended up going to the United States? Why didn't we go to Israel?" Dad said, "We had no choice. We took the first visas that came our way and then we were on our way. Whoever gave us the affidavit that made it possible to come to the United States first is the one we chose."

We were allowed to take out four boxes packed with belongings, silver and china. A lot of people smuggled money out of Germany. My father decided not to risk the lives of his wife and kids by doing that. While the boxes were being packed, a Gestapo goon watched what was put into them. My father plied him with schnapps. I remember the moving van taking our belongings to the railroad station in a carriage drawn by two horses. I was also given a ride on the carriage to the station. When I visited Lippstadt several years ago the railroad station hadn't changed at all. There were no more horse-drawn carriages but the mood of my memory was still very strong. These pungent memories flooded my consciousness as I stood seeing things as they had been.

As we left Lippstadt for the last time, the most inhuman screams that I have ever heard in my life came from my Grandmother Hirsch. She knew that they would never see us again. But she said, "It's all going to be all right. We will be protected by God and the German government."

My father's uncle in Hamburg invited us to stay with him while we waited to embark on the ship to America. We took a train to Cuxhaven because the ship *New York* couldn't get into the shallow harbor at Hamburg. Before we arrived at Cuxhaven, the door of the railroad car opened and an *SS* man slammed the door into the compartment. He yelled, "Let me see your visas!" Father gave him all our documents. After a few moments the man's face softened and he said, "Thank you, *Heil Hitler,*" and slammed the door behind him. It's very tough to recall these memories. This was truly one of the saddest days I experienced.

We boarded the ship and Mother became seasick before the boat left the harbor. I have tried to think how my father and mother must have felt leaving their homeland with $200 and two Leica cameras. I don't remember how many days it took to cross the ocean, but it seemed never-ending. We were berthed in steerage, which were tiny cabins facing the interior of the ship with little air to breathe. We stopped

Ralph Eichengrün, Paula Eichengrün, Paul Eichengrün, Walter Eichengrün
On board ship *New York* 1938

in Southhampton and Le Havre, but we didn't get off the boat. This was about four months before the War started. We were well on our way to the new land. Mother and I were seasick, but Ralph and Dad felt spry and excited.

My father had built a life for his family and had to change all his concepts. He was 42 years old at the time of our crossing the ocean and I suspect that he saw things the way my grandparents had. If he hadn't had a family I suspect he would have tried to chance it out in Germany. For a freedom-loving American that sounds odd, but for someone who grew up in Germany it doesn't sound so strange. I remember being placed on a box so I could see from the deck of the ship as we passed that beautiful lady, the Statue of Liberty. You can't believe the joy we felt. Our parents had carefully taught us what the statue stood for, just as they had carefully warned us about the election in 1932 being the last free election in Germany. They left their homeland

and went to a strange country and they just plugged away in order to make it.

I want to pay homage to them for the courage they had, and what they did to leave Germany. What I really mean is that a lot of families stayed in Germany and ended up in Auschwitz. My parents, because of their foresight, decided that neither they nor their kids should die.

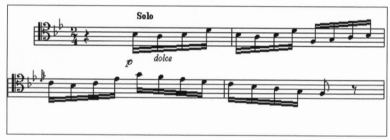

—from Beethoven *Symphony No. 4*

Chapter 2
New York, San Francisco, & Salt Lake City
1938 — 1944

As we approached the gangplank to disembark, we heard our cousins barking like dogs. "There they are," our cousins waved and screamed as they spotted us. We had made arrangements for them to let out a loud bark to identify themselves. Having immigrated earlier to the United States, our cousins were now living in Mount Vernon, New York. We had a lot of relatives living near New York City. As we drove to their home, I remember passing a fruit stand that seemed to me to have at least a hundred thousand oranges on display. I felt I was in a dream. There is a book written in German called *Schlarafenland,* which is about unimaginable, imaginable situations. It is a book about some kids who have to eat themselves through a wall of chocolate pudding in order to get to the other side. Driving to our cousins' home and seeing all those oranges reminded me of that book.

We stayed with our cousins a couple of weeks while Dad and Mom looked for work. Remember the four cases of belongings that we had packed in Lippstadt to take with us? Upon arriving in New York, the American customs officers broke most of the china that we had brought from Germany. I remember my mother sitting there in tears holding Grandmother's china, which had been cracked and broken. The sea voyage hadn't been so rough and the packing had been completely German. Packing is something Germans do to perfection. Why? Who in God's name can explain that kind of destructive behavior? It was a truly cruel act.

While my parents looked for work, my brother and I lived with a cousin in the Bronx. In the evening the elevated subway line made a screeching right turn at our bedroom window, leaving us sleepless most of the night. New York seemed to me to be very dirty and dark. I hadn't seen Park Avenue, Fifth Avenue, and 76th Street. In reality it may have been quite different, but that was my mood at the time.

I didn't speak a word of English. Rescue came in the form of the YMHA (Young Men's Hebrew Association). The YMHA had a summer camp at Bear Mountain, which was very near New York City. They asked me to stay at the camp for six weeks. Everyone at the camp was Jewish, and learning English brought me out of my depressed state. Believe it or not after six weeks I was fluent in English. Must have had something to do with my musical ear. The kids and counselors alike took special care of me.

During this time my brother Ralph was busy going to summer school and he also had a part-time job at a service station. He bought a piccolo from part of his earnings— and that's where the story really begins. It seems I was very jealous of Ralph for having such a wonderful new toy, so whenever he wasn't at home I went to the closet and sneaked out the piccolo to play it. I was pretty good after a few days of screeching on the instrument.

New York was *so* different from Germany. I couldn't believe that the chamber music concerts in the museums were free. Ralph and I listened to the Metropolitan Opera radio broadcasts on Saturday mornings, and we also listened to the NBC Symphony under Toscanini on Saturday afternoons. On Sundays we heard the New York Philharmonic under the direction of Bruno Walter. Sunday also brought us Fred Allen and Jack Benny.

Finally, my father found a job selling imported delicacies and sweets to Jewish homes in Westchester County. He needed a car for his business and bought a Willys for $50. I remember six months later he traded that car for $55, then he had another car, then another. To Ralph and my great delight he finally bought a Ford with a rumble seat in which we sat with joyful glee.

But Dad had great difficulty learning English, because there was no one to teach him the language, and sometimes this caused great embarrassment. I went with him once when he was selling these imported foods. We went to this lady's house and rang the door bell. The maid answered and he said, "May I talk to the lady of the house?" The maid said, "I'm sorry, but she's passed away." "Vell, ven vill she be back?" was his response. That kind of stuff. It hammered him down after awhile.

My parents just hated New York, because they were living on such a limited income. Every month, in order to make the rent, they would sell some of the silver they had brought from Germany. That ran out pretty quickly. So Dad said "We can exist here for only a short while. The furthest place from New York is San Francisco. We'll go there." The Council of Jewish Women gave us enough money to buy the bus tickets for this journey.

We packed our belongings and took a Greyhound bus to San Francisco. The trip took four days and four nights and was pure torture. In San Francisco I remember walking with suitcases from the bus station at Seventh and Mission Streets to the Jewish Agency on Divisidero Street. It was quite a hike. The ladies at the Agency sent us to a boarding house. We had a terrible time in San Francisco. Dad couldn't find any work because so many Jewish refugees were coming into San Francisco from Shanghai. These were immigrants who had come out of Poland and Russia.

There was a lady in our boarding house who was deaf, blind, and couldn't speak. My brother and I learned sign language from her. We took her all over San Francisco and spent a lot of time at the World's Fair, which was located on Treasure Island. At the time I was 15 and my brother was 17. The blind lady paid us a small amount for keeping her company so we were able to make a little income for my parents. Also, after school I would jump on the street car at Tenth and Market and go one block, sell newspapers and make change for the customers, and then jump off. Whenever a private car came along Market Street I would jump on and off the running boards. People who bought the paper from me in this perilous position were really helpful and kind.

However, six weeks of that routine was enough for me and I was more than ready to accompany my family when they decided to move to Salt Lake City. With no real income in San Francisco, my dad became depressed. If there had been work, he would have stayed there. He took English lessons from a nice Jewish lady, but without a job that didn't help the depression too much. Eventually he did learn English.

It took Dad three months to find a job in Salt Lake. A Jewish-owned supermarket offered him work as a night watchman. So Dad took the job and we were on our way to Salt Lake City. The women from the Jewish Agency met us at the bus and welcomed us. They took us to an apartment, which they had filled with furniture and delicious food. These dedicated ladies were absolutely wonderful to us. I remember my mother sitting in the apartment, crying in relief; the tension from those six last years in Germany, plus beginning in the United States with new difficulties had taken its toll. We lived two apartment houses away from Brigham Young's grave.

Salt Lake is a beautiful city, surrounded by high mountains, and I was so happy when we arrived there. To be in such beautiful surroundings really gave me a lift. Before this time I had tried to play all kinds of musical instruments but was not very successful. I played the flute for awhile. It didn't appeal to me. In Salt Lake City the junior high-school music teacher suggested that I play the oboe or piccolo. I didn't like the oboe either, and stopped playing it as soon as possible. Then I chose a piccolo because I wanted to be in com-petition with my brother, who played the flute.

Paul Green 1943
Naturalization Certificate photograph

But my love affair with music really started in high school, in tenth grade, when my music teacher, Mr. Billeter, said to me, "Open the door of that storage closet and you'll see two Heckel bassoons. Would you like to try to play one of them?" The bassoons were excellent and I loved the feel of them in my hands. He said, "Put the bassoon together and here's a reed. Soak it up for me and play a few notes."

Mr. Billeter decided that I should play the bassoon and the moment he placed the instrument into my hands and I heard the sound, I instantly knew that this was to be my future in high school, music school, and the professional world. Little did I know that I would become principal bassoonist of the Utah Symphony, Indianapolis Symphony, and finally the San Francisco Symphony and Opera!

Talk about tunnel vision, I really had it. Most good Ameri-can kids wanted to be bankers and lawyers, but I wanted to become a bassoonist. I just knew I had to play the bassoon and do it professionally. There was this incredible eagerness to do a good job, to make a sound that pleased my ears and to bring myself to some kind of musical satisfaction. This

Walter Green 1943
Naturalization Certificate photograph

satisfaction lasted through to the last note that I played in Mendocino 60 years later.

I told my mother one evening when we were walking, "I am going to become a professional bassoonist because that is an instrument that truly fits my needs and being." Her response was, "Wait awhile, you're a little bit young. It's too early to make such a big decision." I said, "No, this is it! I know it. Mom, I am going to be a professional bassoonist." She was soon very simpatico about her son's musical interests and had nothing but encouragement for me. This was just before the beginning of the Second World War, and there wasn't a bassoonist or a bassoon teacher around, so I had to learn the fingering of the instrument by myself from a method book.

However, if Mr Billeter couldn't teach me how to play bassoon, he covered my other musical needs during those high-school years. He taught me harmony and a very small amount of counterpoint. Mr. Billeter took a great liking to me and I to him. On weekends I would take my bicycle with my bassoon on the rear seat of the bike and ride to his home in the mountains near Salt Lake. A wonderful musician, he could play all the piano concertos of Mozart from memory. I never understood how such a major talent ended up teaching music in a high school. And he taught me about musical style. Audiences have no idea which orchestra is playing, but they learn quickly as they listen to performances. There are as many styles as there are orchestras in the world. It is important that the musicians convey to the orchestra and to the public their own style of playing.

I had no idea of studying anything but music. One day during geometry class I decided to write a symphony. I ended up composing the Haydn 88th. I'm sure Papa Haydn will forgive my plagiarism. I had a lot of fun in high school. Mr. Billeter's son was my best friend. He was a year ahead of me in school, but I was king of the roost, as it were, because of my musical talent. When the music teacher was absent because of illness, I conducted the orchestra, chorus, and band. Along the way I became Drum Major of the West High School ROTC (Reserve Officers Training Corps) Band and we would take the band on a march down Main Street in Salt Lake City. I was in my glory.

A few months ago I started thinking about what brought about my interest in learning to play the bassoon. My folks gave me enough money to buy a record album once a month. My guide to higher musical aspirations was the conductor Felix Weingartner. Once a month I eagerly went to the two music stores in Salt Lake City with the $3 that my mother and father had given me. I went to the music stores to acquaint myself with all the great classical masterpieces. In those days everything was recorded on 78 rpm records. I could listen to my heart's content in the soundproof studios in the music store. I bought a recording of the Mozart Bassoon Concerto. Only one recording of that concerto existed then.

My mother was very worried, as good mothers are, that I wasn't going to make it through high school. I don't know what prompted her to see the principal. My grades in other subjects were triple A. I had almost straight A's in high school. I don't know why she was worried. There's a German phrase, which is *Es gehört zum guten ton:* "All this belongs to a good sound." For the mother to go to the high school and find out how her son, her favorite son, is doing. Well, she went to Mr. Baker, the high school principal, who told her, "Mrs. Green, I don't know why you are here. Walter is my best student." "Oh, I just vanted to know." My mother spoke broken English, but fluently. Her written English was wonderful.Flawless. I haven't the slightest idea why that was. Maybe she studied English when she went to finishing school. I don't think she ever went back to school, but she educated herself in many subjects. She was marvelous!

In Salt Lake City there was a WPA orchestra called the Utah State Symphony Orchestra. The WPA (Works Progress Administration) was a Federal program that created work for artists and musicians during the Depression, which was just coming to an end. The Utah State Symphony played four concerts a year, but didn't have its regular conductor, Hans Heniot, because he was busy with basic training and conducting the Army Band. At age 16 I was asked to play third bassoon in a concert conducted by Sir Thomas Beecham. Beecham was the far-sighted owner of Beecham Pills, a great English patent medicine cure-all. Sir Thomas decided that it would be more comfortable to wait out the war in Oregon and Utah. Sir Thomas turned to the audience in the middle of a piece being played and berated the management of the Utah State Symphony for not having a major symphony orchestra in their wealthy community. Two years later the Salt Lake community organized what is now known as the Utah Symphony (which contained quality players like Walter Green!). During the concerts with Beecham I played third bassoon, which was written in tenor clef. I didn't know what tenor clef was, so I played the whole thing in bass clef, which sounded wrong, and it took Beecham awhile to figure out what was going on. He was very nice to me. I had to learn tenor clef within a week from one rehearsal to the next concert.

High School Graduation Diploma 1944

The Eichengrün family always needed money. When Dad's job as a night watchman ended he was offered a job managing a little clothing store at $50 a week, for ten hours a day. He spent the next twenty years working very hard. Dad's reputation as an honest person was well known. When the Ute Indians came down from the mountains where they were shepherds, they would ask Dad to hold their salaries for them, except for enough money to buy a day's liquor supply.

My non-musical career began in Salt Lake City. Every morning all through high school, I arose to service two paper routes, and I also worked at an A&W Root Beer Drive-In. During the summers I worked at an amusement park named Salt Air, where people could swim and float in the Great Salt Lake. I sold popcorn and ice cream and other goodies and worked myself into a managerial position. I felt sad because I had to work hard while going to school and couldn't even attend dances with my high school buddies and their friends.

After I graduated from high school in 1944, I worked for two months as a packer at the Clear Field Naval Supply Depot, driving Cats and stacking war equipment. After this job I drove a Martha Washington Candy Company's delivery truck, even though I had never learned to drive and didn't have a license.

I was inducted into the Army in October, 1944 at Fort Douglas, Utah, which was on the edge of the Wasatch Range. The sergeant lined us up, showed us how to stand at attention, and said that all men who had been in the ROTC should take three steps forward, which I did. He smiled at us and said "You are all on KP duty tomorrow." The second day in the Army I spent peeling potatoes. I quickly learned the most valuable lesson of my life—don't volunteer for anything while in the army. I don't know how the army trained us to become such vicious infantry men!

In basic training I learned a lot of things, including the fact that the people who were training us were trying to turn us into monsters. This was infantry basic and what they needed was cannon fodder. You became a monster, because you knew how to stick a bayonet into a dummy sack or jump across a creek and end up in the middle of it. I was a platoon guide for a while. After sixteen weeks, we had a ten-day furlough, and then we were supposed to go on to a port of embarkation. I went to Salt Lake City to say goodbye to my parents and then hopped on a train and took myself to Baltimore, Maryland.

In Baltimore, we had a few days to mess around and to entertain ourselves. We were given more shots, new uniforms, and new rifles. I felt pretty well equipped. It never occurred to me that I could be shot and killed. It just wasn't in my character. I was no hero of any kind. If I had to take a shot at a German, I don't know that I would have. I really thought about it a great deal. It had nothing to do with patriotism. It had everything to do with a humanitarian position and survival.

One afternoon at a Servicemen's Club (USO) outside Baltimore, where you could play cards and talk and eat doughnuts, I heard some beautiful music. I went over to the record player. Somebody was playing parts of *Der Rosenkavalier* and I said, "My God! Are you doing *Rosenkavalier*?" He said, "Yes, we have a recording here with Lotte Lehman singing it." "It's wonderful!" I said. "Are you a musician?" "I hope to be," he answered. His name was Bob Lehrfeld. We became buddies and went overseas together on the *USS America*, which was then a troop transport. I said, "Do you play an instrument?" He said, "Yes, I play oboe." "I play the bassoon," I told him. I had not had a lesson up to that time.

—from Mozart *The Marriage of Figaro*

Chapter 3
Italy, Austria & Germany
1944 — 1946

We boarded the troop transport *USS America* and headed for the rough waters of the Atlantic Ocean. Red Skelton, the comedian, was on the ship. He entertained the troops on the way over to Europe, then tried to console the wounded on the voyages back. That was his job during the war. Bob Lehfeld and I just enjoyed each other's company. My God, in the infantry, you didn't get the cream of the crop—you got the cream of the crap!

As we neared Gibralter, some British destroyers came racing towards us and began to drop depth charges. I was up on A deck, high up on the ship, and I became very nervous, which I hadn't been before. Somebody said, "Want a smoke, Green?" "Yeah," I answered, "Let me have it." I smoked two packs a day for the next twenty years just like my dad. But I did eventually give it up! We weren't torpedoed. We saw the Rock of Gibraltar, then sailed into the Mediterranean Sea and ended up in Naples, Italy. There were a lot of *fascisti* running around, shooting people, even though the Allies were mostly in control. They set some bombs off in the Naples Post Office.

Bob was still with me when we disembarked and we carried our duffel bags into the Army trucks that were waiting to take us to the Army base. The camp where we were billeted had been the ranch of Count Ciano, Mussolini's son-in-law. It was now a German prisoner-of-war camp and every six or seven nights Bob and I had guard duty. I would march up and down one side of a street and Bob would march on the other side of the street. We thought it was terribly boring. We'd meet in the middle and begin singing Beethoven's *Fourth Symphony*. We'd both start at the same point in the symphony, singing our way down my street and his street and then we'd come back. When we met we'd see how far off or on we were. We were always very close, since we were two really intelligent, wonderful musicians. It was great! We had it right more often than not. By the time we marched three or four times down the street one movement would be finished. I don't think we woke up the German POWs. Those wonderful vocal shenanigans were ours to remember for all our lives. It so happens that Beethoven's *Fourth Symphony* contains one of the most difficult bassoon solos in all of his nine symphonies. It's just a technical thing, but it has bugged me all through my life.

We had a wonderful time doing that, as well as getting vino from a nearby farmhouse. Bob and I would go on forced night marches just to keep our bodies in good shape. We would duck out of the column, pour the water out of our canteens, put vino in, then walk the rest of the staggering miles to get back to the base. There was nothing much to do. It wasn't a pleasant duty and anything like this helped to buoy our sagging spirits.

We had a company commander who was just a total jerk. I understand that a couple of weeks after I left the outfit he got "fragged," was shot and killed by some American soldier. I understand that this sort of thing happened often to commanding officers, but I was never in combat, so I really don't know.

We were waiting for orders to be moved to the front. President Roosevelt had died two months earlier and we were within a few weeks of the end of the war. Mussolini was hanged and we saw some gruesome photographs of *Il Duce's* body. One day I received a call to come to the office and was told to report to a Captain Ringel. I saluted and set my course for the officers quarters. I had no idea what the gentleman had in mind. Could it have been the wine in the farmhouse? Upon reaching the Captain's office, he said to me, *"Rüht Euch."* I said, "I beg your pardon, sir?" He repeated, *"Rüht Euch."* I said, "I'm sorry, I don't understand." "What's the matter, soldier. Don't you understand German?" I replied *auf Deutsch*, "I think I understand German and speak it much better than you do, sir." He surely understood that and looked at me sharply and said, "That's all, soldier. Dismissed!"

Three or four days later came another call. "Green, pack your bags. You're going into another outfit. And use a cover for your name and destination." Then I realized that Captain Ringel had learned his German in the U.S. Army Counter Intelligence Corps. *"Rüht Euch"* means "At Ease" in German. I said goodbye to Bob Lehrfeld, but I would see him again later in my life.

I packed my belongings and went to Casserta, which is just east of Naples, a very picturesque town. There were two outfits there, the British Eighth Army and the American Fifth Army. General Mark Clark was the commander of the American Fifth Army group. The officer in charge called me into his office and said. "Don't salute. We don't do that here." And then he said, "Green, I understand you're a Communist!" I said, "I beg your pardon, sir." "I understand you are a Communist." said the officer. "I'm sorry, sir," I replied. "I didn't know that."

Evidently, the FBI had checked me out in the States. In high school I had been part of an after-school study class of different political ideas. We studied the Communists and we studied the Republican Party, the Democrats, and all other forms of political activity. It had been school-sponsored. I explained this to the officer in charge and he dismissed me saying, "Okay, Green, go to the Royal Horse Stables where you'll find the mess hall and a place to sleep."

The camp where we were stationed had been King Victor Emanuel's summer palace.

The next few weeks were glorious. I must have drunk eight to ten cups of tea a day with the British trainers. What they were training us for was basic counter intelligence. If you were really high up in intelligence work you went for training at Camp Ritchie, Maryland, which was sort of like the World War II CIC (Counter Intelligence Corps). OSS (Office of Strategic Services) was another branch of the same department. This was military intelligence. Allied forces—American, British, and French—occupied what would eventually become West Germany and Austria plus parts of Vienna and Berlin. The headquarters of American Territory was the I. G. Farben building in Frankfurt, Germany.

We actually learned very little in Casserta and mostly helped put boxes of cards into the trucks. These boxes contained small cards with the names and addresses of Nazis—German Nazis, Austrian Nazis, British Nazis, Russian Nazis—with details about what they had done in their years of service. I don't know how in the hell our Army intelligence got those cards. They were files that Eisenhower called SHAFE cards. SHAFE was an acronym for Supreme Headquarters Allied Forces in Europe. We kept loading and loading these cards.

Once the trucks were loaded we sat on the top of the trucks and guarded these valuable cards across Italy and into Austria. We drove up from the boot of Italy all the way to Salzburg, which was our first stop before going into Vienna, to the Vienna Mission. We had a fabulous time. There were five or six Army trucks, filled with these cards. A lot of stories on those cards have never been told.

Two of the officers sitting on the truck were Colonel Crowley and Captain Ringel. Captain Ringel spoke four or five languages fluently. In civilian life he was a judge in New York City and after the war he wrote the definitive books on the Fourth and Sixth Amendments of the U.S.

Constitution. He became a friend of mine for the rest of his life, a wonderful human being, beyond belief. When he died two years ago, Judge Ringel was 94 years old.

We had a wonderful staff. Henry Pleasants, after his stint in Army intelligence, became music critic for the *Philadelphia Bulletin* and later on wrote many books about music. He was a lovely man and incredibly intelligent. Another was a Mr. Hein, who was a conductor of one of the orchestras in Munich. One captain had taught ancient history at Brown University. And I come into this milieu? Can you believe it? It's like somebody was guiding me through all of this, even though it's all coincidence. These men all spoke German. That was the big deal. I think what all these men had in common were languages. They all were more mature than I was; I was still an 18-year-old.

During the trip the staff sergeant on top of the SHAFE truck asked me, "Green, what is your name?" I said "Walter Green." "No, no," he said, "you must have had another name. I knew a Green in North Africa when we were fighting there." Then he became thoughtful. "It wasn't Green, it was Eichengrün." "Yes," I said, "My name was Eichengrün when I lived in Germany." Then the sergeant said, "Let's see, there's an Eichengrün waiting in Salzburg where we're going to be billeted."

And sure enough it was my cousin, Dan. Imagine, all of this happening six years after I left Germany, and the guy who comes out of the house to help unload the truck is named Dan Eichengrün. Every Eichengrün is related to every other Eichengrün and although I knew Dan's father, I had never met Dan himself. The last person we saw in Germany was Dan's father, who gave us refuge in Hamburg until we got out onto the ship. (After the war, Dan met his wife Lucille in New York where she was living with cousins, and married her there. Lucille had been in concentration camps during the war and survived. She wrote a book, *From Ashes to Life*, about her experiences in the camps.)

32

The second Friday after I arrived in Salzburg Colonel Crowley asked if I would like to become the mail clerk. This job consisted of going to the railroad station twice a day to pick up mail, then delivering it to the soldier boys. He said, "Can you drive a car?" I had never driven a Jeep. "Certainly!" I said. So the first time I drove the Jeep I banged into something with my bumper and bent it out of shape. I told the Sergeant, "The bumper is out of shape, in case you want to know." I learned to drive the Jeep and kept busy delivering the mail.

Then something amazing happened. One of my many cousins walked out of nowhere into my life. That was Martin Mendel, my cousin from Los Angeles. He had looked through Army registers, found my name and what outfit I was with, and came to visit from Zell am See, where he was stationed. We had been raised together as small children. What a wonderful reunion. So now there were three of us in Salzburg: Dan, Martin, and myself. Then the next day, as I was carrying a bunch of mail in my hand, I turned around and there was my brother Ralph. Ralph was stationed in Pilsen, Czechoslovakia as a non-commissioned officer. So the four of us met without my ever lifting a finger to find out where they were stationed. Martin and I had been in contact with each other in the States, but Dan Eichengrün had never met us before. After he left Germany as a young man, Dan had ended up in Cuba before coming to the United States. Although Dan and I had been brought together in Salzburg, my cousin Martin and my brother had been really on the hunt for me. It was unbelievable! That same kind of coincidence had supported my life ever since childhood. It was really like someone looking after me. There's a German, and Yiddish, word, *beschert*, which really applied to me. It means "gifted."

The four of us celebrated being together in Salzburg by buying a keg of beer from the brewery. We had nothing to punch it open with and we couldn't get the cork out so we

Dan Eichengrün, Ralph Green, Walter Green, Martin Mendel 1945

found a big steel bar and stood there with basins ready to catch the beer off the ceiling. It was wonderful beer. We spent the next three days together, finding out about each other's parents and how they came to the United States. During these three days, we had a ball in the incredibly beautiful city of Salzburg, which was untouched by the war.

Martin stayed with his outfit for quite awhile and we corresponded on the teletype while I was in Vienna and he was in Zell, and became best friends forever. There were personal things that happened to us as brothers and as cousins. We kept our relationship going through the years. Dan died several years ago. Martin and I are the only two that are left. His sister, who became my brother's wife, lives in Detroit.

Walter Green, Martin Mendel 1945

More amazing wonderful events kept coming my way during this period of my life. Someone told me they had heard about a bassoon for sale: "I was at the Salzburg Mozarteum and I heard that a gentleman who is quite ill wants to sell his bassoon." I rushed out to find him.

The man who owned the bassoon was very close to dying. I said, "Do you want to sell your instrument? He said, "What I need is food for my family." After the end of any war, hunger is one of the main enemies and people suffer. "How much food would you like?" I queried. "Whatever you can get." he said.

I went to our mess sergeant and asked, "How many K rations can you give me?" "How about four cases?" I said, "Great!"

We didn't eat K rations; we just tried them out. They consisted of Spam,packaged powdered eggs, a chocolate bar that you had to eat slowly, and powdered milk, which

Walter Green, Ralph Green 1945

was Godawful. But they would keep you alive. You bet! Plus four packs of cigarettes.

I took the K rations and gave them to the gentleman, saying, "Is this enough to trade?" "Whatever you have." he replied. I said, "Four K rations?" He couldn't believe it, because K rations were the best of the rations. I understand he died two weeks after we made contact.

So I bought my first bassoon in Salzburg. The instrument was rather old, but that didn't bother me because it was better than nothing.

One day the U.S. Army cadre had a barracks inspection. I had the bassoon lying on my bunk bed and the sergeant came in and said, "What's that lying on your bed, Green? You are not allowed to have weapons in here." I just smiled and nodded my head at him. He walked away shaking his head. He thought I had a bazooka there!

We were stationed in the former Gestapo headquarters. It was part of my work to become "Officer of the Day," which meant that I had to spend a night every month awake near the teletypes. If something urgent, something of real importance, came up we would take it to a higher command. Once, while I was sitting in the office feeling bored and bugged, the teletype went "bing bing bing." It was a communication from Munich (which was in the American territory) to Salzburg. I answered, "Okay, what is it?" He said, "The Bureau of Standards has just announced that the condoms used by men and officers in the Army are defective." Then the guy in Munich said, "Bing bing bing—now he tells me!" That actually happened!

The office in the Gestapo headquarters contained every issue of the anti-Semitic Nazi paper *Der Stürmer*. Some nights I had nothing to do except to sit there and look at the teletype. I spent all of one night reading through every issue of this horrible paper. I used to see these papers and the monstrosities they made of the Jewish people on every street corner in Lippstadt. It was very hard to take and cost me several nights of sleep.

I really didn't do much intelligence work in Salzburg. One of our officers who was in charge and who wanted to impress himself on our commanding officer chased a guy who had spent the night with a beautiful Austrian *fraulein*. I also chased him down and after talking with him found out he was just an American GI who was having a good time. Fraternization was not allowed with the Austrians. We had Servicemen's Clubs and they were supposed to entertain us.

In those days the teletype was the fastest way to communicate. In August of 1945, orders finally came that said, "Next week we're going into Vienna to take our part on the border. You'll love being stationed there." It was very much like Berlin—the four-power idea. There was an agreement between the Russians and the French and the British and the Americans to divide the city of Vienna. The Americans didn't take Vienna. That's the point. They were given it, so the Russians wouldn't take it all. The Russians were there already because they captured Vienna after the war. After a month the Americans, British, French, and Russians took their agreed-upon parts of the territory. We wondered whether we would be able to hold Vienna. We felt truly isolated. Most of the Austrian cities and towns were in the hands of the Russians, but they had agreed at the four-power meetings to eventually give them back to us. The United States managed to convince the Russians that they ought to pull back. We wondered if we could keep the Russians from doing something foolish. Remember the movie *The Third Man* with Orson Welles? It was very much like that.

We came into Vienna on top of trucks with all those SHAFE cards. The city was not in a shambles, but the Opera House was gone. The Alliance Insurance Company housed the intelligence unit of the Fifteenth Army Group. Travel and Border Control was my specialty. We were also part of the occupying army of the United States in Russian territory. There were Russian troops in the city as well as British, French, and American occupation troops. We went to meetings to ensure cooperation between the four powers and to make it safe for everyone. There were very few incidents, really. The only thing I remember is that an American soldier shot one of our greatest twentieth century composers, Anton Webern. I like his music very much.

My work in intelligence really started in Vienna. SHAFE cards were organized by the Dewey Decimal System. It was very boring, but sometimes interesting work. A few times we had weekly meetings with our Russian allies as well as the other occupying armies. The Border Control was very important, first in catching Nazis, but secondly for just being there, to hold on to what had graciously been given to us by the Russians. We had meetings with a British general, a French general, an American general, and a British lady officer. We started work at 8:30 in the morning, worked until 11:00, and then had a little brew. The woman officer was so concerned a-bout my being so young to partake of hard liquor that she always ordered a glass of milk for me!

Once I was asked to speak to and entertain a Russian officer at a party. We had to deal with the Russians once we came into Vienna, the same setup as Berlin. After the fifth shot of vodka I was quite soused. My dear friend Louis Hasbrock ran me around the block three times believing that would sober me up. The Russian officer was under the table, and I didn't feel so good the next day.

I wore enlisted men's clothing except for when I had to interview or in-

Waltter Green in the Vienna Woods 1945

terrogate a Nazi suspect. Then I wore officer's clothing because the Germans and the Austrians had respect for authority. If you didn't have an officer's uniform on, or if you didn't act like an officer, they wouldn't give you any information. But they were so respectful of rank that we just dressed up in officers' clothes. Even though I wore an officer's uniform part of the time, my rank was actually Sergeant, T4.

What happened was that we lost the peace because the Russians became our enemy, although we had been friends during the war. I really think that we should have kept more troops in Vienna, but General McNarney, who followed Eisenhower, let people go scot free, including a guy named Hauseger who supposedly had ghost written Hitler's *Mein Kampf*. Hauseger had been under arrest, but he found a way to escape. The first time I heard about it was when I read an intelligence bulletin. When they let him out he left and then was tracked again on his way to some other place. The story was kind of veiled in the bulletin. I said, "What's he doing free?" And nobody knew. Not one person thought it was important enough to follow up on this amazing tale. If the Nazis were incarcerated by us for a couple of months, they would be let loose! There was no court. You think about the Nürnburg Trials, and that was really a very tasty clean way of taking care of these awful Nazi monsters. But it was largely symbolic. They cut off the tip, but not the top.

There was a scientist by the name of Albert Szent-Gyogyi, who was well known for his work with Vitamin C and cell metabolism. He won the Nobel Prize in Medicine in 1937. We received a proposal through the teletype that Szent-Gyogi wanted to travel to Switzerland. After looking his name up on the SHAFE cards, I saw that he had a very low number, which meant he was a big Nazi and had joined the party in the early 1930s. I sent a message back on the teletype that he did not have permission to travel. This happened at the beginning of 1946. Szent-Gyogyi made a big fuss and contacted General Mark Clark, the Commanding General of the American Forces in Austria, who was his personal friend.

General Clark came into my office and I jumped up and saluted, foaming at the mouth because this great man was coming to talk to a lowly turkey in the army of the U.S. He said, "Who sent this cable?" "I did, sir," I replied. He asked, "Who's the officer in charge here?" "I am," I said. "No, no, I mean who is the officer in charge?" "I am, sir!" What had happened by that time was that American soldiers were leaving Vienna and going home, so we were terribly understaffed. "Soldier," said General Clark, "Let that man through immediately." So we lost the peace, because of events like this.

We all felt like super sleuths doing this kind of intelligence work. A couple of times we were involved in de-

Nazifying the Vienna Philharmonic Orchestra. How could you do that? How can you really tell what a man's inside is? Herbert Von Karajan was not allowed to conduct from 1945 to 1947. I was there in '47 when he conducted the Vienna Philharmonic. The orchestra played the *Radetsky March* by Johann Strauss (the elder), an ironic selection for such an event, as the music had been written to symbolize the military might of the old Hapsburg monarchy.

I didn't like the Austrians in the first place, but secondly, they made such a demonstration about their nationalism that all the things that we read about nowadays—about Austrians being anti-Semitic and being anti-this and anti-that—are really true and had been there long before we ever got there. But I love Vienna. I adore it. I know awful things happened there. I know good things have happened there. And I don't think the attitude of the Viennese has changed a whole lot since that time. Anti-Semitism was pervasive and people were quite cruel to each other while I was there.

But life was good for us in Vienna. While in Austria, American troops could purchase seven cartons of cigarettes a week. I saved most of mine, even though I was smoking at the time. I wanted to take a trip to Switzerland. But one day Henry Pleasants, who was one of the heads of the intelligence unit, came racing down the stairs to me. He said, "Walter, look, in the Vienna paper it says, 'Man wants to trade a bassoon for an AC-DC Phillips radio.' Do you want to buy a bassoon?" I said, "Yeah, but I don't have an AC-DC Phillips radio." "Well, use your imagination, man!" he said. "Get some of those cigarettes and cut out your trip to Switzerland." So I traded cigarettes on the black market. Seven cartons of cigarettes equaled a lot of Austrian schillings. You could trade cigarettes in exchange for that AC-DC Phillips radio, which could then be traded for the bassoon. The bassoon in question was a Kohlert bassoon, not the very best, but it was all right.

So I had seven cartons of cigarettes, which would buy you more than a cup of coffee. What people did was convert occupation money into real dollars. People had Austrian schillings and they wanted American dollars, then you'd convert the schillings back into dollars and come away with a fistful of money. I never did anything like that. Frankly, I was just too scared. I thought if they catch you at it, you're in trouble. It's just not worth it. That way the intelligence helped me. It was okay to trade the cigarettes. I had traded food for the first bassoon that I bought in Salzburg, and the radio for the second bassoon in Vienna.

It was an interesting life in Vienna. I heard so many wonderful concerts, both by the Vienna Philharmonic and the Vienna State Opera. There was a conductor there about whom I knew little, whose best friend was Hugo Burghauser, who later on became one of my teachers. This conductor was Richard Strauss, the greatest twentieth century German composer, who wrote works like *Don Juan* and *Death and Transfiguration*.

I could not believe my good fortune. I thought, "Boy, this is going to lead to something good." And it did, by what at the time was probably an outrageous act. Imagine me as an 18-year-old, coming to Vienna in the Army, putting a bandolier of ammunition across my shoulder and going down to the pit of the Vienna State Opera! I walked up to the principal bassoonist of the orchestra, Professor Öhlberger, and said to him, "You would like to give me bassoon lessons, wouldn't you?" He looked at my guns and said, "Of course!" For many years he had been the principal bassoonist of the Vienna State Opera and the Vienna Philharmonic. He was a very warm and understanding man and a great bassoon teacher. The Vienna State Opera was not playing in its own home, since three American incendiary bombs had destroyed the beautiful Opera House because the Nazis stored their ammunition in the basement.

The orchestra had then chosen to play in a very small theater, the *Theatre an der Wien*.

I bought a lot of wonderful books and things in Vienna. I had a photo engraving of Mahler's *Tenth Symphony*, with all of his handwritten commentaries as to what he couldn't finish and what he was kept from finishing, because he had to sail from Vienna to New York while he was writing the work (which was left unfinished). It had his writing on it. This was a unique copy, supposedly one of only 24 in existence. I bought another paper in Alban Berg's handwriting, with congratulations to Arnold Schoenberg at the first performance of the *Gurre-Lieder.*

I was ordered to take some documents to Osnabrück, which was the headquarters of the British Field Security Service. It's like our intelligence. There were groups of Nazis in all parts of Germany and Austria and I was to deliver their names and addresses to the English headquarters. It would be a long trip, as Osnabrück is about 500 miles north of Vienna.

It was also an opportunity for me to try to find where my grandparents were buried. We had been notified by the Red Cross that they had not survived Theresienstadt. Some distant, older relative, who had survived the camps, had brought the news to Swiss companies, who then made the story into statements of fact, wherever they could. My grandparents, Rosa and Max Hirsch, evidently were deported at the end of 1941, at the time of Pearl Harbor. My grandmother had suffered a stroke and she and Grandad were deported by wheelchair to Theresienstadt. It was a hell of a way to go to a concentration camp. Any way is a hell of a way when the road leads to Theresienstadt. It was the camp for older Jewish people. They stayed there for about a year. They died in Theresienstadt, mostly from starvation.

Anne Frank also went through there, before she was sent on to Auschwitz. Theresienstadt was where the musicians were, and I have a recording packed with beautiful music composed in that camp. The artists and musicians who were in Theresienstadt experienced the last horror before the end. It seems that Germany had been blossoming one last time before Armageddon.

I had the use of a Jeep and an Army driver to go with me to find the whereabouts of those lovely old people. I put some K rations in the back of my Jeep and underneath the K rations were hidden the documents that were to be delivered to Osnabrück. It was a three-day trip to get there from Vienna. The Jeep was winterized with special sidecovers built for Jeeps by the Steyr Autoworks in Czechoslovakia so they could become regular vehicles.

My buddy, Arnie Geier, was also looking for his grandparents. Arnie wasn't going with me on this trip, but we agreed to meet somewhere in the middle of Austria. There are two Linzs: one where my grandfather came from, Linz am Rhine, in Germany, and Linz on the Danube, in Austria, near Vienna. We met at Linz in Austria. Arnie had fashioned a big sign on the side of his Jeep that said, "Hello, Walter." I had to back up a hundred feet or so, because I couldn't stop the Jeep in time with so much snow and ice on the road. We had passed each other going in opposite directions.

My driver and I arrived in Linz and needed more gasoline. At that time, there was a shortage of gasoline for the Army because of some union problems in the United States, so we had to stay in Linz for a couple of days. When you were stuck somewhere like this you would just go into the Army headquarters, find out where the billets were, and get yourself tucked away for a day or so.

From there we went to Salzburg, then on to Munich. We were again short of gasoline, so the next day, just at daybreak, we snuck into the motor pool and stole ten gallons of gasoline off one of the trucks. And we were on our way again. After the documents were delivered to Osnabrück, we drove to Lippstadt, the town where my family lived during the early years of the Hitler era. Lippstadt was in the British territory of Germany.

We drove into Lippstadt, parked the Jeep in the marketplace in the center of town, and put on our dress uniforms. I was wearing a bandolier of ammunition and sidearms. Then we went to see friends of my grandparents. Mrs. Bamberg was the lady who took care of Grandma at the worst time. This was after *Oma* had had a stroke and had to be pushed around with a wheelchair, even into the concentration camp. Mrs. Bamberg had helped my grandparents until the last moment. She was a courageous woman, truly one of the righteous gentiles. I walked up to the Bambergs' apartment and rang the doorbell. Mrs. Bamberg opened the door and saw the ammunition across my chest. *"Ich habe doch nichts getahn!"* ("I haven't done anything bad!") I said, "No, you haven't done anything! You have done wonderful things for us. Frau Bamberg, I'm Walter Eichengrün. The last time you saw me was six years ago." She just broke down and cried. She kissed me and danced me around the room. She was so happy to see me and hear of my parents' survival.

I hugged her and said, "How is Ruth?" That was her daughter. "Oh," she said, "remember when you used to play 'band,' and march around the backyard when you were little kids? One of you played one imaginary instrument and the other played a different one." "Where is Ruth now?" I asked. "She's going to the Conservatory of Music in Lippe Detmolt," which is a small city fairly close to Lippstadt. The River Lippe goes through both towns. I asked, "What is she studying?" I thought she would say the bassoon. "Oh, she's studying piano."

No such luck! Nevertheless, it just seemed amazing to me that both of us were the same age and had grown up together, that I left to go to America and then came back to hear that this former girlfriend of mine was also studying music. It was somehow fulfilling a dream we both had as children.

"Frau Bamberg, did any Jewish people return from the camps?" "Only one," she answered, "Erna Sostheim." Out of a population of maybe 100 or 120, one Jew had returned from Auschwitz and Bergen-Belsen. Erna Sostheim had lived through Bergen-Belsen, and then was brought back to her home in Lippstadt. Mrs. Sostheim was a very close friend of my mother and I was delighted that she survived.

I decided to go look for my mother's dear friend. As I went in the direction given to me by Mrs. Bamberg, I noticed a British soldier walking up the street. I asked, "Could you tell me where *Lipproder Landstrasse* is?" He gave me the answer in broken English. I was surprised and said, "You are a British soldier." He said, "No, I belong to the Palestine Brigade and I am looking for my aunt." The Palestine Brigade was a group of British soldiers who were Jewish, and had performed magnificently in the Second World War. Later on this group of soldiers became the officers of the Hagganah.

Mrs. Sostheim was deeply moved by our coming to visit her. She knew me as a little boy and I had been at her home for coffee and kuchen and also supper on occasion. I asked her, "How are things for the Jewish people here?" She said, "What Jewish people? I am the only one that returned. We were arrested and put away into concentration camps and we mostly died there."

Looking at this wonderful woman's face I thought, "We have to do something extraordinary here," especially when she told us about the graveyard: "The Jewish graveyard is in terrible condition, with no flowers or nice bushes. The gravestones are knocked over and the Christians are growing tobacco on the graves."

The Palestine Brigade soldier and I decided it was time to correct that miserable situation. We did that by kidnapping the *burgermeister*, the mayor of the town of Lippstadt. We drove to the Town Hall in our Jeep, pulled out our guns, and walked into the mayor's office. "Are you the mayor?" He said, "*Jah*, what can I do for you, gentlemen." I said, "Come with us," and we put him in the back of the Jeep and gave that SOB a very tough ride through as many potholes as we could find.

When we arrived at the cemetery, I said to the mayor, "If you do not clean this mess up in one month, I won't be responsible for your health." The Palestine Brigade soldier said to the mayor, "You know, you can't leave the living in peace and the same goes for those who have died. I won't be responsible for what happens to you if you do not respond positively to our plea." A month later my mother wrote to me that a letter she received from Frau Solstheim said that the Jewish cemetery was in perfect order.

We tried to look for my grandparents' graves in Lippstadt, but we couldn't do it. It brought back too many memories. All I could do was go to that graveyard. There was nothing else to do.

While in Lippstadt I met Gerhardt Schreiber, who was Jewish. He came from Anrochte and used to go with me to our *cheder*, the "Sunday School," every Monday. Now he was in British Intelligence. Schreiber asked, "Would you like to arrest anyone? I don't know how long I could keep them incarcerated, but I could do something." "Yeah," I said, "I'd like to arrest *Lehrer* Witte, who hounded me whenever I participated in his classes." Herr Witte was the teacher who used to be invited to our home for the Sabbath meal, which is a great tradition in Judaism. Schreiber said, "Let's go. Take your revolver with you. It's enough." "Where is he?" "Working in the drug store on the corner," he replied. "Let's go."

Schreiber told me what to say after I got in there. And there he stood—the monster! The one who had thrown the medicine ball at me. The man who threw me off a slide into the water and almost drowned me. Lovely guy. I said, "Bring your toothbrush with you." Witte turned every color of the rainbow and then back again. "Come with us," I repeated. "I haven't done anything!" he said. "*Lehrer* Witte," I said, "you must surely remember some of the things that you tried with me and did to me." I put handcuffs on him and off we went to the jail. I don't know what happened to him afterwards. They probably let him go after 24 hours.

Later that day we heard that the British Field Security Service was looking for us because we had done things we weren't supposed to do in British territory in Germany. I thought it was time to high-tail it out of there. We started on our way back and left our friend from the Palestine Brigade at his post in Una. Then I drove on to Cologne. What happened to me in Cologne is probably the most poignant memory recorded in this book.

My driver (the other American soldier who was with me on the entire trip) and I rested for the night in the British billets in Cologne. It was early afternoon, about 3:30 p.m. We found something to eat, some bangers and mash. I decided to look for a family who had been my best friends and my parents' best friends, until we left Germany. I had spent a great deal of time with them, when I was living in that large city. They were Mr. and Mrs. Isaacson. Their daughter was my first girlfriend, when I was nine or ten years old.

The British Red Cross in Cologne gave me the address where my friends had lived six or seven years before. I had brought the Isaacson's address with me from the United States. I went to the apartment house where they had lived. No one had ever heard of them.

I went back to the Red Cross and they said, "Let's look it up in the files, Sergeant." They had the information. It turned out that the Isaacsons had been put on a transport by the Nazis that had never reached its goal. The train disappeared from the face of the earth. This suggested that it probably was put on a siding and burned, with all the people inside. It was late in the war when that happened. The British forces had the information quickly at hand, so I knew looking further for them would be futile.

What I thought of was the incredible pain that those people must have felt, dying like that. And I finally grasped that I could never understand six million deaths, but I can understand one. I knew about the six million, but I *understood* for the first time, about one, my girl friend. She was on that train.

Holocaust victims—The Isaackson Family 1938

That was, for me, a most profoundly uplifting experience—that I could finally understand what one death meant, although I would never truly understand what six million meant. What this story is really about is what it takes to understand the tragedy, and to somehow make your peace.

Chapter 4
Salt Lake City, New York City, Rochester, Salt Lake City
1945 — 1952

After a year and a half the Army decided to discharge me. We took a troop train from Vienna to Cuxhaven, a hospital train with Red Cross markings all over it. We sailed back to the United States on an Army transport ship. It was most amazing, coming into New York Harbor, going past the Statue of Liberty a second time. The whole thing was wonderful, particularly that I made it home with no injuries.

We disembarked in New Jersey. Before I went home I had one thing on my mind. I was invited by my best buddy's parents to spend some time with them in Newark. Arnie Geier's father was a cantor in the Jewish synagogue in Newark. I had helped their son. He had spinal meningitis while we were in Vienna and I'd been able to procure penicillin, which was then a new and rare drug, from the black market. I took Arnie to the hospital just in time for him to make it past the Grim Reaper. He was so sick, my dear friend, that he had to stay back in Vienna. Spinal meningitis is a horrible disease.

As I arrived at their house I saw banners hung along the street, because the family felt so grateful for what I had done for their son. They spoke a little German and a little Yiddish, and they truly showed their gratitude to me. It was a wonderful day. Arnie was not a musician, but he loved to play honky-tonk piano. His enthusiasm was infectious. Later on in life he wrote about insurance and became a millionaire doing that kind of work.

After I returned to the Army camp, I took a train to Fort Sheridan, Illinois, an unusual ride because we traveled in cattle cars. The Army had blankets and foam rubber mattresses for us. We rode through the hinterland of America. Before we were discharged, we immediately sat down in front of a stack of papers that we had to fill out in triplicate. It was like no one could spell, or like the Army intelligentsia were not that intelligent. I was glad to get finished with it all. At Fort Sheridan I was asked if I would be interested in continuing work in Intelligence. Being tunnel-visioned as I was, I decided it was really not for me at all, that I could do much better playing the bassoon. I really knew what I wanted to do—there was no question about it. I did look over the papers, but I realized that what I did in the Army was not something that I wanted to continue doing.

My trip to Salt Lake City was marred by two incidents. Twice I was challenged by the Military Police. The first time, I had my discharge button on and told the M.P. that I wasn't in the Army any more. He smiled and said, "Lucky you." The second time, when I got off the train to get a sandwich, without wearing a hat or a tie, an M.P. came up to me and said, "Soldier, you're out of uniform." Pointing to my discharge button I said, "Who are you calling soldier?" He muttered something and walked off.

When I returned home to Salt Lake City, I was met at the train station by my joyful parents and my brother. Many of the soldiers from my outfit had fought in the Battle of the Bulge and didn't make it home. The Army had selected me for intelligence work because I spoke German. They'd been totally mistaken in picking me, a mere 18-year-old. The usefulness of my German was marred by the fact that I didn't speak the Viennese dialect. Oh my God, the Viennese

Walter Green 1946

accent is thick! I never learned to imitate it.

Dad hadn't had a car since New York and my parents needed one. I had $300 in my pocket. We bought a Hudson, a car that's no longer made. I loved helping my parents out of their poverty.

Shortly after returning to Salt Lake, I decided that I should go to a good music school. My father said, "Go to the University of Utah. It's good enough for what you want to do." That really did it. That got me out of Salt Lake. Mother said, "No, no, go to New York and I'll go with you." My mother was surely the most wonderful human being that I ever knew in my life and so supportive about my playing an instrument. She just turned herself inside out to say good things about what I was doing. It was just beautiful, and she was a beautiful lady. She was so incredibly helpful in my ambition to become a musician that she wanted to go with me to New York to guide my progress. But that was really an impossible request, and my parents and I had a very bad scene. I said, "Absolutely not! If you want to go, go, but not with me!"

I saved my life that day. A few years later, in college, my roommate and I were in a movie theater and we saw one of our teachers. He was very much tied to his mother and we saw them both sitting there, stunned, because what they had just seen and digested was Eugene O'Neil's play, *Mourning Becomes Electra*. My buddy and I were almost in hysterics, unkindly so—but it's the sort of thing that could have happened to me.

In the late summer of 1946, I applied to the three outstanding music schools: Eastman, Curtis, and Julliard. My first choice was the Curtis Institute of Music in Philadelphia. It was a great conservatory for many reasons. One reason was that during the First World War, by an odd coincidence, there were three woodwind players stationed at the Great Lakes Naval Base, north of Chicago. They were J. Walter Gutter, Marcel Tabiteau, and Vincent Pezzi. Their style of playing influenced all of America and the rest of the world. Marcel Tabiteau was the principal oboist and J. Walter Gutter the principal bassoonist of the Philadelphia Orchestra, and Vincent Pezzi was principal bassoonist of the Detroit Symphony and the Rochester Philharmonic. Because Leopold Stokowski and Eugene Ormandy kept that beautiful sound in the Philadelphia Orchestra, these three woodwind players made and taught that great sound at the Curtis Institute. And Marcel Tabiteau had a huge influence on double reed playing. But I didn't get to go to Curtis because I was too old, at 20 years of age. If I hadn't been in the Army I would have been young enough to go there.

I was accepted at Julliard and Eastman for the following year, and I had to choose between them. I chose Eastman because I thought I would feel more comfortable in Rochester. The Julliard School of Music, located in New York City, had a feeling of too much high pressure. I chose Eastman because it seemed to have a more gentle style of studying. I auditioned with Hugo Burghauser in his New York apartment. He prepared me for my entrance to the Eastman School of Music.

While I was in Vienna, I had taken lessons from Karl Ohlberger, the man who I went up to wearing the bandoliers of ammunition. After a year, when the Army was about to send me home, Karl Ohlberger decided that I should continue my studies in New York with Professor Burghauser, who was the contra bassoon player of the Metropolitan Opera. My bassoon studies would not be interrupted and I would continue to learn the Viennese sound. The Vienna Philharmonic's bassoon section was proud of its sound and Ohlberger wanted me to bring that tradition to the United States, specifically to New York. I could go right on with a different teacher, including making my own reeds, and continue the Viennese style.

That's why, when I went home to Salt Lake City, I started thinking about moving to New York. I had Burghauser's address and got in contact with him. He said, "When you get here, come and see me." Before 1938 Professor Burghauser was principal bassoonist of the Vienna Philharmonic. He was very interested in continuing the Viennese style of bassoon playing, which was not the American way. Hugo Burghauser had been the best friend of Richard Strauss. He was a lovely man, a cultured individual who before 1938 was the *Vorstand* of the Vienna Philharmonic, the personnel manager of the orchestra. That was a huge job because Viennese orchestras are state subsidized. He took care of business for the men in the orchestra.

Even now, when I hear very old recordings with Ohlberger, I cannot believe that this man played everything on the Heckel bassoon. The Viennese sound is heavy and dark. Mozart never heard the Heckel bassoon, but there was a man by the name of Almenrader who helped Heckel to elicit a sound that is much closer to what we hear today. Mozart wrote a *Concerto for Bassoon and Orchestra* (Köchel 191), and he also wrote a piece for two bassoons (Köchel 192).

I arrived in New York via Greyhound in the fall of 1946 and began studying with Professor Burghauser. He was delighted to have me as his student. I lived on the West Side between 176th Street and Amsterdam Avenue, in the part of Manhattan that we used to call the Fourth Reich, because of all the German Jews who lived there. You could hear as much German on the street as you could English. I also started working at Macy's in the Children's Department, scooping ice cream. My room cost $10 a week. I went to Chinese restaurants for my major meal, which never cost over 75¢—the dollar was much more valuable than it is now! My job paid $40 a week. The dollar amount stuck with me all my working days in New York. Money, as always, was tight and my GI Bill wouldn't begin until I was enrolled in a school.

Then I was hired by the Gerben Painting and Decorating Company. I walked around large factories in Long Island, and then called the owners up to tell them they needed a paint job. A number of factory owners availed themselves of this particular painting business as a result of my phone calls. But then there was supposed to be a very large painting bid placed for City Hall in Manhattan. I overslept and was too late putting in the bid from Gerben. They gave me hell, but they didn't fire me, because they felt that this youngster had a nice personality, who brought in jobs for them. They were pretty sad when I resigned a few weeks later, because I was offered a free place to live.

Some distant relatives of mine, Bea and Eddie Hermann, wanted me to live with them while I was studying with Professor Burghauser. I had my own bedroom in their home and I baby-sat their two children once in a while. Bea's father was a Fuller Brush man and her husband, Eddie, was chairman of the New York Chapter of the Jewish War Veterans. Living with the Hermanns was uneventful, but very nice. While I was in their home I learned I had been accepted into the Eastman School of Music. Living there, I had the peace and quiet I needed before taking auditions to get into Eastman, and the feeling of being cared for was wonderful during this time of preparation. I was practicing at least four hours a day, even with the little children about—which was difficult, but not impossible. I attended concerts of the New York Philharmonic, standing room only, of

55

course, because I couldn't afford tickets. New York is a very busy city and just thinking about it now makes me nervous.

There was a new principal bassoonist of the Philadelphia Orchestra, Sol Schoenbach, who followed the great J. Walter Gutter. I wrote a letter to Schoenbach while I was still in Vienna that said, "The bassoonists in the Vienna Philharmonic are out of cane. They are playing on reeds that are 50 years old and won't vibrate any more. They have no way to write to southern France, where the farmers grew the cane used to make reeds. I would be glad to pay you if you would send us some reeds." I wrote this as an American soldier. He replied with a very nasty letter that read, "After what they've done to us, I should help them by sending them cane! No way! But come and see me when you get back." I had also told him that I wanted to study bassoon, so he was going to take me as a student. He was probably a good teacher, but I didn't go to see him. I had had enough of his attitude. I saw people dropping from hunger on the streets in Vienna during the winters of '45 and '46. I can argue either side of it. Mostly I don't like the Germans of that period. (That's an understatement, if I ever read one!)

I went cold turkey to Eastman and the Dean of Students welcomed me warmly. I was given a place to live, which, of course, I had to pay for, but we had the GI Bill. It didn't cover everything, but it helped us along and my parents simply didn't have the money to help me. I borrowed $100 from them when I left Salt Lake. Once I was in New York, I didn't go back to Salt Lake City. It cost money—even on the Greyhound.

At the end of August the school opened for freshmen. I'm saying "for freshmen" because as music majors we had to take a series of short tests of our abilities, which wasn't done in any other school except Eastman. They had song sheets ready for us and in between the tests we would all sing *Songs from the Auvergne* by Canteloube, which was a wonderful way of relaxing. It is beautiful music. As we sang from the song sheets between tests, I remember wondering if I would make it. Nobody had asked me for anything like that before and, quite frankly, I don't even remember what the songs were about, so it became unimportant. But it was important enough for them to test us even to find out where we should sit in the orchestra, which is very important if you are a fiddle player and there are 32 violinists in the orchestra. These weren't auditions, they were just tests. In all the years that I auditioned for orchestras, no one ever asked to see my degree from the Eastman School of Music. Musicians don't care about that. They absolutely don't!

One of the good things about the Eastman School was that we had to take university courses as well as courses in music. However, you never saw students from the other departments as we were isolated in the music school. The regular university was out of town, but the Eastman School was in downtown Rochester, which didn't look very inviting. I know there was a Burger King right nearby and a burger was 10¢, 20¢ for two burgers, and we did have to count our shekels like that.

The first year was heavily centered on architecture. Our final test in that subject was that we had to take our notebooks and go through the hall of the school and write down all the different architectural designs in the vaulted ceiling, which was uniquely, wonderfully beautiful. This had a big effect on my music making. Every piece of music that one plays has an architectural content, and it becomes an integral part of one's playing.

We had an absolutely wonderful teacher, Charlie Riker, who made a big impression on us all. He taught English, Poetry, Ethics, and Aesthetics. He didn't teach music. We took his classes at his home. There were ten of us. He'd fix us each a martini—a big stiff one—and made us a wonderful pork roast. Then after that, we would talk about aesthetics.

Walter Green and Bassoon 1948

The next morning we'd all meet for coffee and donuts. Mr. Riker was a wonderful teacher and they were wonderful donuts. He was probably the best teacher I've ever had about anything. We trusted him and he trusted us. And even though he didn't teach music, he would play piano for our recitals; he was a very fine pianist.

I think Eastman Rochester was a very unique place. I don't know what it's like now. I haven't been there for 50 years. They invited all of us who had graduated to be in the Rochester Alumni Association, but that didn't take me back to Rochester.

My bassoon teacher was Vincenzo Pezzi. He had such a big heart for us that he often invited the bassoon class to his house for dinner on Sundays. We'd walk in and there was a picture on the wall and Mrs. Pezzi would say, "Hey

Walter, come in. You lika da picture? That's the Moonlight Sonata! I'ma gonna go now and play the bingo." In those days the older ladies would go to church to play bingo.

Mr. Pezzi was in his late fifties when I was at Eastman. He was my teacher for four years. I would practice four hours a day and practice until I would drop on the floor. I would come in for a lesson and be totally shot before we even started. Mr. Pezzi would say, "Hey, Walter. You got any brothers and sisters?" "Yes, I have a brother." "What does he do?" "He is a doctor," I would say.

He would look at me for about three minutes, which made me squirm in my seat, and then he would say, "That's a nice profession!" Which meant, "Get the hell out of here. Don't ever show your face again."

Vincenzo Pezzi

At least I felt it meant that. But he did it in such a way that it had a huge effect on me and other students also.

When Mr. Pezzi retired, David Van Hoesen took his place as the bassoon teacher, and he has been a marvelous educator. He produced wonderful bassoonists, including the principal bassoonist of the New York Philharmonic, Judy Leclerc.

My piano teacher at Eastman was Harry Watts. We teased him about his name and started calling him Vladimir Harrywatts. It was all done in fun. You weren't being paid to play, but you must understand that coming out of the Army, and into a high-pressure conservatory, made us love our profession even more.

I also took German to get extra credit. I had an agreement with Mrs. Kneissel, who was our German teacher, that I didn't have to come to class. That was in my first year and it fulfilled the language requirement. It was very important to learn German because much of orchestral music is printed in German.

We had a French horn teacher by the name of Arcadia Eugoodkin who was a total character. With his wife on his shoulders, he walked out of Russia in 1917 and came to the United States just after the revolution. He became principal horn of the New York Symphony under the great conductor and composer Walter Damrosch. That was not the New York Philharmonic; it was a whole different orchestra then. We called Arcadia Eugoodkin "The General," because he walked around in a morning suit and spats. He used to talk about the teacher of Heifetz and all these wonderful artists in Tsarist Russia. "The General" would mimic, "He's up there catching flies." He was a truly great horn player.

We had these characters in Rochester who enriched the school culturally. Actually more great teachers came out of the Eastman School than performers.

In my first year at Eastman we were asked by the University of Rochester to play with a wind ensemble at a football game. But the class of 1951 was not interested in football. One of our great "wind-musicians-pretending-to-be-football-players" ran onto the field and caught a pass from the opposing team. We were never invited back. Frederick Fennel, who started the whole concept of wind ensembles at

Eastman, was very upset because it didn't fit into his paradigm. He was a very good conductor, and he especially enjoyed conducting Mozart. If you look in the literature, you'll see that Mozart excelled above all his fellow composers with wind ensembles. He understood more about wind music than any other composer of the eighteenth century.

Mr. Riker had started a settlement school in Rochester where the kids could go after school, to learn an instrument and to study with me and people like myself. At one point the music department placed a notice asking if anyone would like to repair bassoons. Of course I answered the ad, thinking of dollar signs. I was hired to overhaul eight bassoons, and it was a Godawful mess. I must have done a horrible job. There are things about the bassoon that are very technical and very difficult to adjust correctly, in order for it to stay adjusted. Everything tends to want to shift. You have to get to a fine bassoon repairman to take care of an instrument that needs to be tuned like a watch. A good bassoon repairman that I know is Jim Laslie in Indianapolis. He has repaired my bassoon for many years.

But nobody ever found me out. It takes many hours to learn to repair an instrument. It's not that hard, except that you need a lot of patience and fortitude. To seat a pad to cover a hole, the pad has to be a certain thickness and it takes time to be seated correctly. This is a way of tuning a bassoon. I hadn't learned that at the time, and I apologize to the Eastman School for not knowing enough. I never told them. I would have owned up if I had to, but nobody ever asked me, and you can get desperate because if you're running out of your last penny, it can get to be pretty awful.

The reason the Eastman School of Music had good bassoons was because Mr. Pezzi had made certain that whenever they bought a bassoon, they bought a good one. A good Heckel bassoon, in those days, cost $800. Today one would cost $35,000. I sold mine recently. It was a very heavy part of my life to let go of, something that had been my partner for so many years.

The last three years in school I roomed with two very dear friends, Robert Klump and Peter Berquist. Bobby Klump studied flute with the principal flutist of the Rochester Philharmonic He was the most beautiful flutist I've ever heard. At the end of the school year, Bobby and his teacher would play duets backwards, just because there was nothing else to teach him. He ended up as piccolo player in the Saint Louis Symphony, which was a relatively small job. Before his retirement, he taught music in a college near Sacramento, which has a very good music department, including a teacher who studied bassoon at Eastman while I was there. I lost touch with Bobby, unfortunately.

Peter Berquist, my other roommate, became head of the Department of Musicology at the University of Oregon. He has been in my thoughts for many years and we hope to see him this summer on our vacation trip. He's a very fine human being.

I was an ordinary student in the school and people would say I played okay on the bassoon, but what I can't explain is that those people who made straight As were never really heard from again after they left school. I keep thinking of the concertmaster of the Metropolitan Opera, Ray Geniwick, who was not well known at Eastman but who made it big for many years. Ray is a wonderful violinist and he had proved this quality at Eastman without notoriety. His wife, Judith Blegen, was a leading soprano at the Metropolitan Opera.

In my second year, the Eastman Placement Bureau arranged for me to have jobs with the Syracuse and Utica Symphony Orchestras. I played four concerts with each orchestra. I would take a train from Rochester, stop in Syracuse, and then I had another stop later on in Utica. They were community orchestras and, as such, reasonably good.

I remember coming in to a rehearsal of the Utica Symphony and I had forgotten my music stand. We had these collapsible wire stands. I went up to the conductor and said, "Sir, I'm Walter Green." "Oh, glad to have you with us, son." He was an elderly man. I said, "You don't happen to have an extra music stand, do you?" He sat down and gave me a lecture on what I needed to have in order to be a good musician. I had to have an instrument, first of all; I had to have a good reed. And he went down the list and I got a real kick out of that—you know where! It was a good lesson to have the music that is going to be played as long beforehand as possible, and to include a wire stand in your bag of tricks.

Our repertoire consisted of the following: Tchaikovsky, Brahms, Schubert, Schumann—mostly German repertoires and the classics. We were not into modern music at all, mostly because smaller orchestras like those simply couldn't afford to hire an extra musician. If it took three bassoons, you'd do it with two. I learned repertoire there, plus I earned $50 for each rehearsal and $50 for the concert, and there was even some food money. These people really treated their musicians well. With that and the GI Bill, I made it, with an occasional stint as a Checker Cab taxicab driver when I ran out of money. This way I was able to keep myself afloat. Our needs were different than they are today.

Utica and Syracuse were small towns then and the community orchestras were more flexible. Accordingly, I could experiment and see how my tone would go in one direction or another direction or if I added a vibrato or if I played straight or if I played a little louder or a little softer. I made a reed a little differently, because making reeds was 60% of bassoon playing. I learned to play music that I had never known or played previously. This was most important, that I should have the ability to know orchestral repertoire.

I was delighted to have another way to earn a little money, but then the reality of stage fright took hold of me. It lasted the rest of my life. I didn't know about it until it appeared while I was playing my third professional concert. I've never been able to shed this anxiety, but it made for wonderful music. Nothing in particular brought it on. The conductor was very nice to me and I remember the head of the music school in Syracuse said I had the most beautiful bassoon tones made by anyone. It was during an opera rehearsal by the American composer, Norman de la Joio. His presence didn't bring on the anxiety—that wasn't it. I've gone to shrinks and that didn't help either. I've had acupressure and acupuncture and none of it helped, ever. I had to learn to play with anxiety. I guess that professional musicians are made to deal with anxiety. I fought my own heroic battles.

The one person who helped me was Bruce Beach, a very dear friend. I watched him play a concert one afternoon. He was more advanced than I was. In that concert was the *Concerto for Two Pianos* by Mozart, I saw Bruce sitting there as principal oboist of the orchestra. While playing one of the solos in the concerto I saw his hand trembling and I realized that someone else had anxieties also. It was helpful for me to see another musician suffer the way I suffered. I think I would like to write a concerto for orchestra and anxieties that would include all of us. Anxieties were a by-product of making great music. And it seems anxieties were more common in my day than now, because these days musicians are trained better.

I have to explain this whole subject. When Roger Bannister ran the four-minute mile, he did it with more ease than anyone had ever done it before, and the reason was because of better training. When some young person is playing the bassoon or any other instrument now, his nervousness is less than in my day. As a matter of fact, it may be less now than it was 15 or 20 years ago. As an example, when I was studying, just to learn to play a scale evenly was enough to throw you out to the wolves—and I am talking about the training in places like Eastman and Julliard. It's much more rigorous now.

Socially, my life was going relatively smoothly. I was invited to spend Easter with my girlfriend at her parents' home in Toledo, Ohio. I liked her so much that I proposed to her. She said "Yes," but then either she or her parents must have thought I was a total schmuck and she wasn't to see me ever again. I am glad I was saved from total disaster.

Another event that happened while I was in school was that a group of graduating students decided that Eric Leinsdorf, who then conducted the Rochester Philharmonic, was playing too much "junk" music. Leinsdorf put the Tchaikovsky *1812 Overture* into one of his programs. A bunch of graduates went up in the loft of the auditorium with old pillows sliced open. When the part came with the cannons, they shook the pillowcases and feathers came down all over the stage. Leinsdorf kept conducting. Afterwards, I'm sure he threw up.

When I was in my second year at Eastman, the second bassoon position opened up with the Rochester Philharmonic, and I played an absolutely lousy audition for Leinsdorf. He didn't take me and I felt very bad, particularly because I would have been able to sit next to my teacher, Vincent Pezzi, for a whole year.

This business of auditioning is tricky. Sometimes you just have a bad day. It got even worse. I auditioned for the Baltimore Symphony, for the job of principal bassoon. Simon Kovar, who was a great bassoon teacher at Julliard and played in the New York Philharmonic, sat in at the audition, where his favorite student from Julliard was also auditioning. I played what I considered to be the best audition I ever played—period. The business manager at the Baltimore Symphony said, "We'll get in touch with you this afternoon, three or four o'clock. We'll finish the thing off. You have the job. You have my word for it!" I was in seventh heaven, eighth heaven! He didn't call and didn't call and didn't call. I had his number so I finally called him. He said, "I'm sorry," he said, but Mr. Weisberg won the job." Such things happened. The bassoonist who came in first is a wonderful bassoonist and years later the same thing happened in reverse. I won the job in the San Francisco Symphony and he came in second.

In my second year at the Eastman School of Music, I took an audition for second bassoon with the Indianapolis Symphony. The job went through the Eastman Placement Bureau. The Eastman Placement Bureau was a busy place, helping students to get instrumental experience. It was wonderful.

The conductor of the Indianapolis Symphony, Fabien Sevitsky, was the nephew of Serge Koussevitzky, the conductor of the Boston Symphony. Sevitsky asked me to play, and the audition was going really well. I was playing one of the Bach *Unaccompanied Suites* when the maestro stopped me suddenly and said, "You sharp." That means you're high, you're sharp. I said, "Okay." When one pulls the crook on the instrument the pitch will go down, because the player has made the bore of the bassoon longer. I started playing again and Sevitsky said, "You still sharp." So I pulled the crook a little bit more. "Why you play sharp?" I made like I was pulling, but I didn't do a thing. "Did the conductor tell you to play higher?" "No," I said. "Well," he said, "you play very well. I offer you second bassoon in Indianapolis." "I'm not taking second bassoon jobs anywhere," I replied. "Why you audition for me when you know it was second bassoon?" I said, "I need the experience, Maestro." I was starting to get chutzpah. "Hah," he said.

I had made a decision not to accept any second bassoon jobs. Absolutely! My roommate Bobby's father, Dr. Klump, had played flute with the Sousa band, the best band in the land, years before. Dr Klump said, "If you don't want to be typed as a second bassoonist, play and accept only first

EASTMAN SCHOOL OF MUSIC

Of The University of Rochester

KILBOURN HALL

THIRTY-SEVENTH GRADUATION RECITAL

526th in the Series of Graduation Recitals

WALTER GREEN, *Bassoon*
ROBERT KLUMP, *Flute*
(Candidates for the Performer's Certificate)
Students from the Classes of Vincent Pezzi and Joseph Mariano

bassoon jobs." I have followed that principle all through my career and Dr. Klump's advice was truly helpful

In my fourth year at Eastman I auditioned for Hans Schwieger, the conductor of the Kansas City Philharmonic. Among other things, he asked me to play a spot in Wagner's *Lohengrin*, which consisted of triplet figures. I screwed that part of the audition up. The rest of it was good and Schwieger went to our Dean of Students and complained bitterly that I didn't know that part in *Lohengrin*, which is ridiculous because you can't learn the whole orchestral and operatic repertoire. It's impossible. And especially in the middle of an opera, the middle of the first act, the triplet section—that is, unless you happened to win the job as principal bassoonist at the San Francisco Opera, which came to me some years later.

Howard Hanson was head of the Eastman School of Music and we performed a lot of his music. Dr. Hanson loved his own works and performed them whenever the occasion arose. His *Romantic Symphony* and *The Nordic Symphony are* wonderful. When I played my graduation concerto (Mozart's *2nd Bassoon Concerto*) with the Rochester Philharmonic, Dr. Hanson said, "My boy, bring that score into me and we'll play through it." I brought the score for the concerto into his room and he sat me down at a music stand. Then he

Howard Hanson, reknowned composer
and Director of the Eastman School of Music

started the introduction to the concerto on the piano and
he was reading it at sight, because he had never played the
concerto before. Not only was he reading it at sight, but he
was transposing it, because the score had the wrong
transposition. He was a superb theorist and musician.

Years later, in San Francisco, I came backstage during an
intermission and there was Howard Hanson, with his little
beard and goatee. Mrs. Hanson joyfully gave me a hug and
said how glad she was to see me. Dr. Hanson said, "Oh yes,
it is so nice to see you again," but he obviously didn't remember me at all. I wish he had said something more honest, but he was pretty old by then and perhaps he wanted
to avoid embarrassment.

Walter Green, receiving congratulations from Howard Hanson,
after performing his graduation concerto (Mozart's *2nd Bassoon Concerto*)
with the Rochester Philharmonic. 1950

Graduation! We sat in the pit and played for the graduating class. The next day the graduates stood on stage, except for Walter Green, who was in the pit. We finished playing the graduation and we went out and had a wonderful meal in celebration. When I say "we," I mean my two roommates and me. That was the end of the graduation. I left this great institution feeling very sad. Eastman has stayed with me all these years and the joy of completing my four years there was a great way to start my performing career.

After my graduation, I went to visit my brother Ralph and his wife, Judith. Judith and Ralph lived in Detroit, where

Walter Green — B.M. *Bassoon.*
Performer's Certificate. Activities:
Phi Mu Alpha; Junior Symphony; Senior Symphony; Phi Mu Alpha Symphonette.
—photograph and description from *Score*, 1951 Eastman School of Music Yearbook

he was doing his residency in psychiatry. On my way to Detroit, about a six- or seven-hour bus trip from Rochester, I felt miserable from some kind of stomach ailment. I extended my stay with Ralph and Judith for a few more days and Ralph, as a doctor, prescribed Coca Cola syrup, which made me well again. In 1951, Coca Cola still had cocaine in it. Yes, it did. Judith and Ralph were both busy with their jobs, so I had a quiet place to myself.

What happened next might make one believe in serendipity. In order to make a little money my mother would bake butter cookies, using my Grandmother Hirsch's recipe. Mother bagged them in two-pound sacks and sold them to people in the Jewish community. One day an order was picked up by Lucy Abravanel, the wife of the conductor of the Utah Symphony. Abravanel was a well-known Jewish name in Spain. Mrs. Abravanel came for her cookies and asked my mother if she had any children. Mother said, "Yes, my son is a bassoonist and he studied at the Eastman School of Music." Mrs. Abravanel asked, "Has Maurice heard him play?" My mother said, "No." Then Mrs. Abravanel said, "My husband needs a bassoonist."

She called her husband at the symphony offices from our apartment and said, "I have a bassoonist here." Maurice Abravanel said, "Have him come over to the office and bring his bassoon." It was for the second bassoon audition, but it was a job possibility. Mom said I could have my old room back, which psychologically was pretty awful.

Paula Green 1948

I went to Maestro Abravanel's office and he asked me to come in. He was one of the warmest and dearest human beings I've ever known. "Ahh, Walter, it is a great pleasure to meet you. Play for me something." He had a French accent. I played a couple or three things from the orchestral repertoire, mostly the cadenzas from Rimsky-Korsakov's *Scheherazade* with big fat solos and from the Shostakovich *Ninth Symphony*, also with a big fat solo. I had those pieces ready for auditioning. Those were big enough solos and cadenzas to keep me busy practicing for many months. The Maestro said, "I'll give you the job, Walter. I will make you my principal bassoonist." The salary was only $85 a week, with no benefits, but I walked out of Abravanel's office feeling jubilant. Maestro Abravanel was a very good conductor. He did a lot of work with Kurt Weill and also conducted musicals on the Broadway stage. The job opening with the Utah Symphony came from my mother's butter cookies.

I thanked my mother very much for getting me the job as principal bassoonist of the Utah Symphony. But I was worried that the Utah Symphony wouldn't be up to my standard, coming from the Eastman School. I became very depressed thinking that I was capable of a better job. Yet for someone to walk out of the Eastman School to a major job was quite an achievement. I also taught at the University of Utah while I was in Salt Lake City.

My mother was just delighted and very happy to have me home. I really enjoyed the job in the Utah Symphony. The wind section was excellent, and the strings were also good. The concertmaster of the orchestra was Jerome Kassins, who preceded me in the Indianapolis Symphony as concertmaster. Jerry and his wife Sophie became my dearest friends. They took me under their wings and taught me something about orchestral etiquette. What I learned about orchestral behavior from them, as well as from experienced orchestral musicians, is that it is best to mind your own business and just do your job.

The Utah Symphony rehearsed and played concerts in the Mormon Tabernacle, which was famous for its great acoustics. The Tabernacle acoustics were supposedly so great that the reverberation of the hall echoed seven or eight times. A guide leading visitors around the building would stop our rehearsals and drop a pin, to demonstrate the magnificent resonance in that hall. A musician always managed to push a music stand over when the pin dropped, which made us all happy to be a part of this demonstration.

One of my biggest thrills when I was in the Utah Symphony was playing the Brahms *Violin Concerto* with Jascha Heifetz. It was total magic. The man was total music! He

Chamber Music Group of the University Of Utah 1952

played so beautifully, so far beyond what anyone else could do. I remember one of our violinists standing outside Heifetz's room playing the Brahms *Concerto* just before the maestro was going to play. Heifetz looked up and raised his brow sarcastically—and he did that like no one else could. I tried to slink away, embarrassed for this guy, when Heifetz said, "Who does he think he's kidding."

Salt Lake City had a very active artistic life. There's a wonderful art museum there and the Mormons gave a lot of money to artistic institutions, including the Utah Symphony. Salt Lake turned out to be a good job, except that I couldn't make a year-round living with the orchestra. Eighteen weeks of work in Utah and that was the end of the season. So I started looking for other opportunities.

That summer I went to Hollywood, where musicians could get pickup jobs. I joined forces with a friend of mine, the principal trumpet of the Utah Symphony, and we took an apartment in the Hollywood hills. Thor Johnson, who conducted the Cincinnati Symphony, was guest conductor for the *Messiah*. Maestro Johnson liked my playing very much and asked me to play an audition for him, which I did. He assured me that if he had an opening in Cincinnati I would be the man for it, but there was a bassoonist there who was very good and had a long tenure.

One Sunday morning I was sitting outside on the apartment balcony enjoying my morning coffee and the telephone rang. I lifted the receiver. "Mr. Green, this is Fabien Sevitzky." I said, "Oh yeah! Sure!" "No, no, this is Fabien Sevitzky." "My foot!" I said, "Who gave you my name and telephone number?" The voice on the other end replied, "The Eastman Placement Bureau." And I knew it was serious. Sevitzky said, "You want play for me first bassoon in Indianapolis?" I said, "I would LOVE to!" He said, "I pay you $125 a week for 23 weeks." That was a start. I said, "Seriously, how did you get my name?" "Never mind," he answered. "You still play sharp?" I said, "No, I don't play sharp any more. I have a different bassoon."

I called Maestro Abravanel immediately and said to him, "Look, I have a chance to play principal bassoon in Indianapolis." That was a higher quality job than the Utah Symphony. He said he would release me from my contract and that I could take the job, so I was very happy to give the news to Dr. Sevitzky. This was in 1952.

Chapter 5
Indianapolis
1952 — 1956

I took the train to Indianapolis because management paid for it. It was a considerable savings. When I got there, I was overwhelmed by that large city, where I had no friends or connections of any kind. I remember feeling quite lonely. All I had with me were two suitcases and a bassoon. I was going to live in Indianapolis, but I had no idea where, so I walked from the railroad station toward downtown, which was practically one and the same. I looked for the first hotel I could find, which was little more than a flop house. I put my bags and instrument down and said, "Now what do I do? I think I'll go to sleep for the night, then think about it some more tomorrow." I found a place open for breakfast the next morning, then decided to go to the symphony offices, which were in the Murat Temple, a Shriner's Temple where we played our concerts. It was a pretty good auditorium, as far as having enough echo to make it sound juicy. The business manager of the orchestra, Allen Meisner, was nice enough to ask me what kind of housing I needed and he sent me on my way up to Twenty-Sixth Street, which since then has undergone many changes. That day I settled down in a rooming house, or so I thought.

Sevitzky welcomed me at the first rehearsal and the orchestra applauded as I came in as the new bassoonist. The men and women in the orchestra were very warm and wel-

75

coming. I was not the youngest person in the orchestra; several other musicians were younger. The bassoon section was absolutely first rate. The third bassoonist, who was kind of a grumpy guy, wondered what kind of bassoonist I was. He played a French bassoon, which is fingered differently and sounds different than the German instrument. I was interested to have someone playing a French bassoon, which sounds more like a saxophone than a bassoon. It worked well as far as the music went. In those days there were still some French bassoons in American orchestras. We all sat down and I put my instrument together. We were playing Tchaikovsky's *Fourth Symphony* that day, which was played often during the 1950s and continues to be a favorite everywhere. My solo spots, of which there are a lot in the Tchaikovsky *Fourth*, came off beautifully, I must admit.

I simply couldn't understand how this wonderful orchestra had been in the background of things. That shows you how much talent there is. Indianapolis, I thought, was a backwater—Indian-no place! There are only so many places and they almost necessarily had to be big metropolitan areas and they had these higher quality orchestras that were nearby: Cleveland, Detroit, Chicago, Minneapolis. As far as the public image, there were tiers, and Indianapolis, by its nature, was going to be below those others. But the orchestra was wonderful, and it still is today.

After the rehearsal was over I turned to the guy who was sitting in front of me, our principal oboist, and it was my buddy in the Army, Bob Lehrfeld. I hadn't known he was in Indianapolis. He had just been hired by the Indianapolis Symphony to become the principal oboist, while I became the principal bassoonist. After the first year in Indianapolis, Bob got the job as associate principal in the New York Philharmonic.

So this was the fifth time that I had met Bob Lehrfeld. We looked at each other and he said, "We've got to get an apartment together." So we went apartment hunting that afternoon, after our rehearsal and some lunch. Food was very good in Indianapolis, when one ate out. The only bad thing was that the restaurants boiled their vegetables until they couldn't be picked up. We looked around and found a wonderful place to live. And it was a wonderful season, too, because Sevitzky was a good conductor.

Fabien Sevitzky had been a Russian silent movie star and left after the Russian Revolution. He was also a very talented string bass player, as much a virtuoso as his uncle, Serge Koussevitzky, the conductor of the Boston Symphony. After he came to the United States, Sevitzky played assistant double bass in the Philadelphia Orchestra, with Stokowski conducting. He also founded a chamber string orchestra in Philadelphia, and conducted the People's Symphony Orchestra in Boston. Koussevitzky no longer played string bass, but he was oiled with a lot of money and he didn't want his nephew's successful and popular conducting talents to compete with him in Boston. So Koussevitzky gave Sevitzky something like $50,000, which was an enormous amount of money during the Depression, to take over another, distant, orchestra, which was Indianapolis. Sevitzky could then have the kind of orchestra he wanted and what he did with it was really very good.

Something Sevitzky had learned while in Philadelphia with Leopold Stokowski was seating. Stokowski revamped the seating system of the modern symphony orchestra. For example, first and second violinists sit together as one section, not first violinists, then second violinists, like it used to be in symphony orchestras from the eighteenth century on. "Stokey" wanted better sound and more cohesive togetherness in playing, and he made it work, mainly through the placement of the strings.

Sevitzky would try this every once in a while and take it a step or two further. These changes could be used for any music. He thought it was great to try it and if it didn't work, so it didn't work. But if it didn't, it was the orchestra's fault. It was never his fault that we played lousy. He would try the original, then he would try something more advanced. He kept trying to improve the sound of the orchestra. I was very impressed by that.

Sevitzky was an absolutely weird person. When he came to concerts he always wore a black cape and the inside of it was red. He would come with a cane from which he could draw a sword. Right out of Paris in the nineteenth century. But he was not an old man, probably in his early fifties when I played with the orchestra. A lot of people hated him, particularly because he was not very nice in his dealings with the women of the orchestra. We had a girl piccolo player. In those days, very few women were in the orchestras, usually only harpists.

Because of the tension in the orchestra, sometimes our concerts were bad, sometimes they were indifferent and sometimes they were great. Once at Purdue University we were playing Mahler's *Das Knaben Wunderhorn*. In the middle is an English horn solo and our English horn player screwed it up so terribly that we all started laughing. We couldn't help it. After this miserable performance Sevitzky walked through the assembled throng. I was still laughing. He came by and said, "Is not funny, Walter. Is not funny!" I was dying laughing. People, I think, get too serious about classical music. It's to listen to and to enjoy. It doesn't matter whether you wear this or that. It's just that you're going to have a good time and you might as well dress up. It was the best performance of *Das Knaben Wunderhorn* that I ever heard. I'm still laughing!

You should be getting an idea of the tension felt by the average musician. I had another roommate named Leonard Lindner. His nickname was Lemuel Q. Lager. We were doing Rossini's *William Tell Overture*, the Lone Ranger theme. Just before the Lone Ranger, there's a big English horn solo.

Lindner played both third oboe and English horn in the orchestra. Just as he was to come in, Lindner handed the English horn to our second oboist, who wasn't playing at that point, and walked out. He was never seen again. He said, "I shake too much. Like an old Ford fender." Those were his very words. He later won a job in Chicago or somewhere.

Once we were preparing for the evening concert by playing the afternoon children's concert. Sevitzky had a very great love for Russian music and I never played Prokofiev's *Peter and the Wolf* better than I did under him. I loved playing the grandfather. At the end of the evening concert, Sevitzky, who spoke very poor English, decided he wanted to talk to the audience and said, "This morning, when I was reading the Wallpaper Journal . . ." At this point the whole orchestra ducked, because we were all laughing so hard, we couldn't hold it in. It didn't matter to the audience.

At another children's concert Sevitzky was conducting the Tchaikovsky *Sixth Symphony* and he had people in the class read the annotations to the music. A young girl about 12 or 13 years old said, "And now the orchestra, under the direction of Fabian Sevitzky, will play Tchaikovsky's *Symphony Number Six,* the *Pathétique.* The reason the symphony is named *Pathétique* is because the opening solo is played by a pathetic bassoonist. I laughed so hard that I almost fell off my chair!

Sevitzky once guest conducted an orchestra in South America, in Argentina. Sevitzky said, "Ven I was in Buenos Aires I liked the orchestra, the orchestra liked me. I tell very funny joke and the orchestra was laughing." And our principal clarinetist said, "Yeah, and I'll bet they're still laughing, too!" These were ways to take the tension away.

One evening we were playing the Beethoven *Second Symphony*, and there's a spot in the last movement where, instead of playing it the way I should have, I played a wrong note. I thought, "Oh my God, he's going to get me now!" Because that's the way he worked with the orchestra. He was a SOB to almost everyone, but for some reason not to me.

He was always nice to me. At the end of the first season, when he heard I was going out to California for the summer, he said to me,"Walter, be careful when you drive to Hollywood for the summer. Don't drive too fast, take good care of yourself." He also gave me a check for $100 and said, "Get yourself a decent car so you don't die in a traffic accident," which was pretty generous.

Before my coming into the orchestra, Sevitzky had made many 78 rpm recordings. Few of these were transferred to LP. During my second and third year in Indianapolis we also made some LPs. One was with Jascha Heifetz, and another was the Katchaturian *Gayne Suite*, which is quite a large piece. It was midnight when we did our 18th take of the *Sabre Dance*. We also recorded Dvorak's *Slavonic Dances*.

Butler College had a very good music department. It was only about five minutes from downtown Indianapolis. Every once in a while they needed an extra bassoonist and since money was scarce, I would take the job, but only as principal. That was one of the first testing grounds. Indianapolis had all kinds of testing grounds.

I also taught woodwind lessons whenever possible, to make some extra money. Once after a concert, just as I was walking out of the Murat Temple, a man came up to me and said, "I have a son who wants to be the world's greatest clarinet player. Would you teach him?" After the first lesson that I gave to his son the father said, "Mr. Green, is my son able to play in a major symphony orchestra when he grows up?" I said, "I'm so sorry, Mr. Jones, I can't make that decision. It's too early." He looked at me and, for his seven dollars for an hour's lesson, said, "Okay, okay, I see money bags in your eyes!" Insulting, to say the least.

I was also a Fuller Brush man for a short time. I remember some kind of a comedy with Red Skelton on the radio about a Fuller Brush man. "I hope nobody's home. I hope. I hope. I hope," he said. That's how I felt and didn't stay in that job very long.

I was paid $125 a week in Indianapolis for 23 weeks. I put in an average of maybe 25 hours a week for rehearsals and performances. I had a lot of free time, to practice and to make reeds. The brass players had it made. I always thought, "My God, the triangle player . . ." One of our percussion players was also the business manager of the orchestra. What you get paid is up to you. The way the pay scale goes in symphony orchestras is that there is a basic scale, which is used for everyone. Everyone gets that same amount. You want more, you go ask for it and see if they give it to you. That's the way it goes, even today.

The way my life worked then is that I would play six months in Indianapolis, then take myself out to Hollywood and find whatever jobs I could get. Taking a job there was illegal because I wasn't a member of the union, so I didn't tell anyone. I didn't receive my union card when I was playing in San Diego because time was against me—I wasn't there long enough to establish residency.

My first job on the West Coast was playing principal bassoon with the San Diego Summer Symphony, with Fabian Sevitzky conducting. Principal bassoonist, always principal. While playing in San Diego, I remember doing the *Third Leonore Overture* by Beethoven and there's a flute and bassoon duet in this work. While rehearsing the *Leonore Overture* I felt quite anxious. At intermission Dr. Sevitzky called me into his room and this time he called me Walter. "Walter, don't worry, it will be all right. We will work hard and we will get it. It will be just fine!"

At the end of the second year I received my union card and played the Ojai Festival. I also played the Griffith Theatre in Los Angeles, where there is a big telescope, and also the Greek Theatre, which goes on about the same time that the Los Angeles Philharmonic plays in the Hollywood Bowl. Griffith Park and the Greek Theatre had beautiful musical concerts. We did two weeks with the New York City Ballet and did the Balanchine version of Stravinsky's *Firebird* with costumes and sets by Marc Chagall. Not bad.

I played second bassoon for those concerts, because I was too hungry not to accept that position. This was my first experience with Los Angeles musicians—first-rate conductors and first-rate orchestras. And first-rate dancers, like André Eglefsky and Maria Tallchief, who were with Balanchine. It was a job with a pickup orchestra in Los Angeles, which was really easy to get. It's not any more, but it was then. If you were an itinerant orchestral player and could get a job like that, you jumped for joy, because it meant four or six weeks of employment. I had hit the big time!

Then the first bassoonist got another job elsewhere, so they put me in as first bassoon. They did that because the assistant conductor of the Griffith Park Opera orchestra, Earl Murray, was also assistant conductor of the San Francisco Symphony Orchestra. He had heard my playing and fell in love with it. Murray decided that he wanted me to audition for an opening coming up in the San Francisco Symphony. Essentially, that's how I got the job. My predecessor, Ernest Koubacheck, had been there for 50,000 years.

Thor Johnson was a very good conductor and was at Ojai that summer. He was the regular conductor of the Cincinnati Symphony. Israel Baker and Jerome Cassins were the rotating concertmasters of the Ojai Orchestra. Jerome Cassins kept feeding me jobs and I received more than I deserved, almost full time. This was beautiful because the pay scale for casual jobs was high. The union brought out a national pay scale and all the men and women of the orchestra were covered.

I also played with the Fujiwara Opera Company, who did Puccini's *Madame Butterfly* with only Japanese singers, which was really beautiful. It was a great opportunity for me, because they asked me if I would go with them on tour. I said, "Until the Indianapolis season begins, in October." "Okay," they said, "We'll let you off then if you help us." Which meant, "If you chauffeur our conductor from place to place." The conductor was Tadashi Mouri and the chauffeur was me, Walter-san. It was a wonderful little trip. We played in San Francisco, Bakersfield, Fresno, all the valley towns. The conductor traveled with me in my car. There were 25 members in the whole troop, but they traveled by bus. Mouri was a very dear man. He spoke enough English so that we could understand each other.

At the end of the tour I returned to Indianapolis. Having bought a car made my traveling much easier. I would stop in Salt Lake City for a few days to visit with my mom and dad, then get back to Indianapolis in time to experience the first snowstorm of the season.

The most important thing that happened in Indianapolis was not the orchestra, but, in fact, my first marriage. There was this lovely woman singing in the chorus for *The Damnation of Faust* by Berlioz, and her name was Charlotte Clark. I needed to talk to her because I had a roommate who didn't have a girlfriend. So I talked with her at the young people's meeting at the Unitarian Church. I introduced her to my roommate, who asked her out on a date, but that didn't work at all. So I thought, "She is so dear. I think I want to date her myself." Then I went out with her and it surely did work because I asked her to marry me after our fourth date.

Charlotte Clark Green was born in Crown Point, Indiana, and she grew up a true Hoosier. Her father was a farmer and he had a really tremendous intellectual capacity, which was mostly developed through spiritual means. She was Methodist, but when I met her, she had become a Unitarian. She was a psychiatric social worker and had a job with the Jewish Family Service of Indianapolis. Naturally, the director of that group was Jewish, but he couldn't find someone who was Jewish to take a new position. On a wild stretch of his imagination he asked Charlotte if she would take the job, and she said, "Of course, I'll do it. Of course."

Charlotte got her Master's Degree at Indiana University. Her roommate in Bloomington was from Lima, Peru. Charlotte was planning to visit her in South America, climb Machu Picchu, and visit several Inca towns in the Andes.

At that time I was playing with the Saint Louis Symphonietta (not the Symphony), which was a pickup orchestra. We had the best musicians, from the Chicago Symphony, the Minneapolis Orchestra, etc. The principal clarinetist was from Eastman; the concertmaster, Erik Rosenblith, was from Indianapolis. In the spring we went on a four-week tour of the Midwest and the South.

One of the places where we played a concert was Notre Dame and the afternoon before we went to South Bend, Charlotte made me a great stew. She went with me and on the way home put her head on my shoulder. We were kids, with naïveté and total love for each other.

Then Charlotte went to Peru for three months. I said, "Be sure you write me every week, so I know where you are and that you're well." I received letter after letter. She had told me before she left that she would let me know whether she would marry me or not. She didn't say, "Yes" after four dates, nor did she say "No." She just said, "I'll let you know." The letters didn't hint at anything; they were just very nice letters, which I treasured. This was after my second year with the Indianapolis Symphony.

I went to Los Angeles for the summer and I played in the San Diego Symphony. Charlotte and I decided to meet in Los Angeles after she came back from Peru, when she would give me her answer. She came off the plane and traipsed down the gangplank into my arms looking more beautiful than ever. She had flown right from Peru to Los Angeles. I found her a hotel room and we spent the evening with some of my cousins in Los Angeles. Later that night we talked about the issue of Judaism. We decided that we needed to talk it out so that nothing would ever come up, that there would never be an issue made over the fact that she wasn't Jewish and I was. Eight hours, in the car, talking it out. The marriage was such that, in 27 years, there were never any disputes about religion.

When I first walked into her parents' home, Charlotte's hundred year-old grandfather, who lived with the family, said, "Say, Walter. I understand you're a Jew. What are Jews like, tell me." So there was no prejudice of any kind. There was just curiosity. Absolutely! The family was very nice to me.

We were married in Indianapolis in September 1954. Charlotte's parents and her aunt Wilma were at the wedding, plus orchestral musicians. The Indianapolis String Quartet played the entrance and exit music. Certainly not Wagner or anything like that, because you know the Wagner. It was a very plain, simple, and wonderful wedding. My brother was my best man. My parents didn't come. I couldn't send them the money at that point and they couldn't afford the trip. Also my mother was very ill. It was an easy trip for my brother to come down from Detroit. Ralph gave me a Seconal to take before going to sleep the evening before because I was so nervous; otherwise I would have been up all night. He took care of his little brother.

After the wedding everybody came to our apartment, which was a converted garage, for coffee and cake. I had to go to work the next morning, but Charlotte and I decided to take a drive down the street. At a fruit stand that I remember so well the vendor said, "What do you folks want?" We bought a sack of apples. I said, "You know, we just got

Walter and Charlotte Green 1954

married this afternoon." "You did?" the man said. "Well, the apples are on me! Have a good life!" And we did. And I did.

Charlotte and I struggled financially because I made $125 a week for 22 weeks—no overtime, no vacation, no nothing else—and then the season was over. The orchestra management tried to find us jobs outside of the music department. I was sent to Allison Jet Engines. They wanted to train me in computers and I asked Charlotte, "Honey, should I do this? Then we'll just get out of the music business." They offered me six months training with a starting salary of $10,000. That was a lot of money then. I didn't do it, because Charlotte said, "Look, when you're 35, and if we're in this position, we'll talk about it again. Until then, you'll do nothing but play principal bassoon." Which I did. That spring I found a job behind the cash register at Hook's Drug Store for $40 a week. A surprising salary! Social workers didn't get paid that much either, and they still don't.

After my third year in Indianapolis, when the performance season was over in April, we decided to go to New York, so that I could apply for a union card. The musician's union in New York City is Local 802. You had to establish residence and wait six months until you received your union card. Both of us found jobs in New York and we lived in an apartment on Long Island. Charlotte became a social worker at the Long Island Jewish Hospital; though she wasn't Jewish she had experience and was very good at it. I found a job in the daytime, taking the social service car and bringing in people who had cancer and needed treatments.

In the evening, at six o'clock, I would be on 42nd Street, which at that time was a wonderful part of Manhattan. I took a course in computers that lasted six weeks, every evening five days a week from 7 p.m. to 10 p.m. I learned a little bit how a collator worked in those days. I trained on the IBM 401 or 402, a hand-driven machine with wiring in the back that used punch cards. After I graduated from the class, they offered me a job at the Shearson-Hammil investment firm. All I did for the next six weeks was to put these cards in order. There was a tray full of cards, but, instead of throwing them in the collator, I did the whole job by hand and ignored the fact that I had just graduated from a course. I was so upset by the whole scene that after six weeks I thought I was going to have a nervous breakdown and I quit. I stayed at the hospital driving the social service cars and with Charlotte working we had enough money.

Then we went back to Indianapolis. That year, 1956, was critical for the Indianapolis Orchestra and for my family and me. Fabien Sevitzky was very serious about everything and not only did he fall in love with a woman who was not his wife—and not so incidentally our orchestra's harpist—but the affair became public knowledge. Mrs. Sevitzky was a big power in the universe of this Indianapolis Orchestra. Most orchestras have someone. She raised a ruckus and, of course, this was Indiana. We were on tour, playing in Baltimore, Washington, D.C., and wonderful halls in Boston and Chicago. While we were playing in Carnegie Hall in New York, the Orchestra's Board of Directors found out about the affair and fired the Maestro in the middle of the season. I was just getting ready to warm up for the Sibelius *Second Symphony,* which has a nice bassoon solo in the second movement, and about to go on for the concert. Sevitzky had just received the word that he was fired. He came down the hall backstage, looked at me and said, "Valter, you are looking at a dead man!" That has been quoted from one end of the country to the other. In April, Izler Soloman took over the Indianapolis Orchestra.

After Sevitzky left Indianapolis, he became conductor of the Miami Orchestra, which was really very low on the rungs of perfection (today it's a very good orchestra). Then he married the harpist, Mary Spalding, and they had a child together. By then Sevitzky was in his early sixties.

When the orchestra returned to Indianapolis, I had a call from San Francisco, asking me to come out to audition. Charlotte was pregnant, due within five days of my taking this audition. I flew on an airplane for the first time in my life. No more Greyhound—that was the end of it. We flew into Chicago, Midway Airport. I stayed there for six hours, waiting for a plane from New York that was going to San Francisco. By the time we got to San Francisco the assistant manager of the San Francisco Symphony, Joe Scafidi, was waiting for me at the entrance to the gate. Twelve, fourteen hours had passed since I left Chicago. As we landed, Mr. Scafidi came to me and said, "Mr. Green, let's go. The maestro is waiting for us." "He can wait," I said, "I need a cup of tea and a cheese sandwich." While I got it, Scafidi growled that we had to go. I said, "Look, I'm tired. I don't know whether I want to play this audition or not, but I'd love to have the job."

I hadn't slept a wink on the plane, I was so nervous. I didn't know what to do, but the tea helped. We went to the Opera House because that's where the symphony performed in those years, up until 1980. I met Enrique Jordá, the conductor of the San Francisco Symphony. He was very nice and put music in front of me to play. I played reasonably well, but it wasn't great playing. First I played solos from every movement of the Mozart *Bassoon Concerto*, then from Beethoven's *Ninth* and *Fourth Symphonies* and from works by Tchaikovsky and Sibelius. I had played most of this music before. A couple of pieces I hadn't performed, but I had fast enough sight-reading ability in those days not to cause me much worry.

The last thing he asked me to play was from Ravel's Second *Daphnis and Chloe Suite*—a beautiful piece. And I thought, "Oh my God, how awful. I played this so badly!" Jordá said, "Would you try it again?" I tried it again and still screwed it up. I thought, "Oh well, the hell with it. I blew the audition. That's the end of that and I'll go elsewhere some time." But Jordá said, "Try it one more time." I did and I got it! It was a technical passage and very difficult. He said, "I tell you what now, Mr. Green. You have the job. You want to talk business with my manager?"

Joe Scafidi and I went into the corner of the room and he said, "Look, I can pay you, as principal bassoonist, $240 a week." Doubled from Indianapolis days! "And," he went on, "after 26 weeks there is a pause, but we guarantee to hire you for the Pops Concerts with Arthur Fiedler. There's four weeks of that." That brought the job up from 26 to 30 weeks. "But if that's not enough salary," Joe continued, "we can talk to the manager, but he won't be back until next Tuesday." "Never mind," I said, "I'll sign this." I wanted it in my hand. I was bleary-eyed, but I was in heaven. I could not believe it, doubling the paycheck and our baby about due.

Then Jordá said, "We have a hotel for you and I can give you a ride to the hotel in my taxi." I sat down in the cab and went "Whewwwwwww!" He said, with a Spanish accent, "Why do you sigh so? You have the job." "I have a baby waiting," I told him.

I called my parents in Salt Lake and they sobbed on the phone. It was just beautiful. Their son had done it. Both sons had done it. This was a reward, in part, for the terrible hardships they had endured during all those years.

I called Mr. Soloman and asked whether he would release me from my contract. I pleaded on bended knees to get out of Indianapolis and go on to a big orchestra, especially because San Francisco still had the Pierre Monteux reputation. Mr. Soloman was a very dear person and said, "I would never stand in your way."

I flew back and stopped in Salt Lake on the way. My parents and I had a couple of good days together. I kept calling Charlotte to see whether the baby had come yet.

Our daughter Nancy Ann Green (Allouche) was born in Indianapolis on May 19, 1956. Charlotte and I were sitting in our little apartment watching a fight on television, with a famous middleweight fighter named Sugar Ray Robinson, and right in the middle of it Charlotte said, "Uhhh, the water broke!" And I said, "Well, let's get ready." And she said, "I'll be ready in a few minutes." "Come on," I said, "I'll get you to the hospital." "Well," Charlotte said, "I've got to wash my feet first." She had been running around on a hot day without her shoes on. I remember being extremely excited that this event was happening, but Charlotte was totally cool. She wrote down everything about Nancy's birth that she could remember and did the whole thing without any kind of anesthetics. She thought that was pretty great. I did too. We all did. Charlotte was such an amazing person!

I built a crib that fit into our new car, a '57 Mercury, which I bought on time—a long time. We put Nancy into it, and left Indianapolis. Charlotte was delighted, except her tears just welled out of her eyes because she had spent so many years in Indianapolis. Hoosier Land was more familiar to her than California. I remember one exciting incident during the trip, because the World Series was on the radio. We were driving through Colorado and we parked by the side of the road, brought out some sandwiches and made a picnic lunch. We left the car radio on and listened while Don Larson pitched a perfect no-hitter. We took Charlotte's parents with us as far as Salt Lake City, because Charlotte's brother lived in Ogden, Utah and they were going to visit him. In Salt Lake we stayed with my mom and dad, who welcomed everybody.

Chapter 6
San Francisco
1956 — 1983

The San Francisco Symphony

C harlotte, the baby, and I arrived in San Francisco and found a small hotel on Geary Street, where we stayed the first two nights. If you ever felt alone with a whole troupe of people, that is how I felt with my wife and my daughter. It was scary. We didn't know what the job was going to be like. We had a little bit of money together, but still it was really scary.

But it's like the gremlins were at work, fixing the next part of Walter Green's life. Within a few days, we went to some rental agencies and rented an apartment in the Richmond district, on Sixth Avenue. A wonderful place, just a block from Golden Gate Park. We didn't have enough money to buy a house yet. We had no money coming in, nothing. We just had to budget and live frugally until after my second year, when we might look for a house.

Charlotte found a job and that's what helped us through the summer. She worked for the San Francisco Adoption Agency, tracing the adoption rights of a parent looking for a child. The rules were very strict in those days; once you gave up a child, there was almost no way of getting that child back. The job paid good money and we could live on her salary. Charlotte was a lifesaver when we were short of money, and she saved us several times during my first few years, particularly throughout the strike by the San Francisco Symphony, when we didn't get paid. During that episode I organized some chamber concerts at the Unitarian Church on Franklin Street, which helped us and some other musicians pay our rent.

Then Charlotte's parents gave a gift of $10,000 to each of their four children. To us that was a down payment for a house. In fact, it paid for a house and a half that included three bedrooms, a social downstairs, a living room, a dining room, and two baths. The house was on Urbano Drive in Ingleside Terrace, right next to Saint Francis Woods, not far from San Francisco State College. The price was $20,000. The land had been a race track many years before. It was a lovely place and when you start thinking about children going to school, or start thinking about having more children, you want a flat piece of land for bicycle riding to keep your kids from flying off the moon. So we were in good shape, as far as money was concerned. We didn't have anything to put in the bank, but we could live on what Charlotte made.

๛

My mother died in 1958. Mom was such a dear. She loved her children, but especially me, her youngest son. I think that created a lot of tension between Ralph and me, because I received the better of things. Mom was the most encouraging person I have ever met, bar none, except for my two wives, who are another story altogether. She was basically a happy person who absolutely adored music. I'd get a little allowance at the end of each month so I could buy one 78 rpm record. She was a generous person in every respect. She was interesting, because she read a lot. My mother was in therapy for seventeen years, which totally freed her from all her troubles. She walked away from it and found a job in the business world and made sure the family had a decent car. She was fabulous.

My father didn't react very well to that. He worked in an Army & Navy store, six days a week, eleven hours a day. When he came home from work, all he wanted was to have his dinner, then listen to people like Walter Winchell and Gabriel Heater on the radio. My father resented Mom going to work. He resented her going to therapy, too. Dad had an old-fashioned idea of women staying in the kitchen. Maybe he resented her success.

My mother was an angel but she and my father didn't have a good marriage. They were married 35 years, because that's what one did in those days. There were no divorces. I don't know why my mother and father didn't get along. Ralph and I often discussed this, but couldn't come to any conclusions, because they were both, in their own right, just wonderful people. It just didn't work. Mom wanted Dad to succeed to such a degree, I think, that sometimes she turned out to be a pain in the ass. He wasn't interested in making money. He wanted to go to shul every Saturday. He was what they called, in German Jewish lingo, a *kovutmensch*. *Kovut* means "Honor." People had parties or coffee klatches and Dad was thrilled when he was there, but when he got home, he became depressed again.

What I want to do in this book is to straighten out some my misdeeds, in terms of the credit my father deserves. As a 42-year-old man, he had to leave his homeland and go to a place that was totally foreign to him. He did everything in his power—and he had a lot of power—to not have his kids or his wife suffer in any way. It was really a masterpiece. When I think how it might be, if I went to a foreign country and had to learn the language and got no credit for it, except that the kids might appreciate what he did for them. I think he was a man of incredible character and a wonderful human being. He never did a crooked thing in his life. He was honorable and righteous, yet depressed.

He was depressed after he left Germany, although he never wanted to go back. A lot of German Jews go back.

Not him. He just wouldn't do it. I remember a time in the early 1930s when he wasn't depressed. I remember very clearly when he was a man of great joy, a happy man who played with his kids. All that disappeared. I took it for granted that this depression wouldn't continue, that he'd get into the stream of things when he had nothing to think about except how to make a living. And it actually did disappear for a while in 1939 when we got to the States, but it came back.

After Mom died, Dad was alone and he tried to get different jobs. One day our telephone rang. I picked up the phone and a woman said, "Hello." For a second I thought it was my mother's voice. But it was my aunt, calling to tell us about her marriage plans with Dad. Aunt Else had a voice just like her sister. She had been widowed five years before. We hadn't been in contact since the two families came to the United States. My mother and her sister had little contact in Germany. There were some hard feelings between them. The competition between the two sisters was very strong. As a young woman Mom played piano and supposedly she played very well. But her parents gave Aunt Else a small grand piano and nothing to my mother. This created some of the jealousy that caused so much grief in both families. They literally did not speak to each other for 17 years. I was named after Aunt Else's first husband, Uncle Walter, who was very successful financially.

Aunt Else lived in Pittsburgh, Pennsylvania, and was in contact with my brother in Detroit. That's how Dad and Aunt Else renewed their acquaintance while he visited Ralph in Detroit. Ralph enjoyed Aunt Else very much. I wasn't so thrilled about her. But Dad and Aunt Else got together and, after the traditional Jewish waiting period of five years, they got married. Dad and Aunt Else had a marvelous marriage for thirteen years. He was happily married to my aunt and became a successful businessman. I'll say this for her, she pushed the right buttons for him to respond like he did. He worked for Goodwill Industries when he was 75 years old. When he was 80 Aunt Else died. Then he married their best friend, Erna Bauer. Four years later, at age 85, he died from cancer, after smoking two packs of cigarettes every day for most of his life.

☙

Charlotte and I decided that our lives were secure enough to have more children and we had two boys, both born at the Kaiser Hospital on Geary Street in San Francisco. David was born on June 12, 1958 and Peter was born two years later, on June 28, 1960. David looked very much like me and like our daughter Nancy, with a lot of dark hair. Peter looked like Charlotte, meaning he was blond. But Nancy looked the most like me and came into the Eichengrün family with a very strong resemblance.

Our kids were the joys of our lives. Charlotte and I were very much in agreement on the way we should raise them, the way we should raise ourselves—that we would stay in a liberal, realistic, fulfilling environment. Charlotte took care of her children in more than a motherly way. That sounds like Gilbert and Sullivan. She was determined that her children would grow up, together with their parents. We all had a ways to go and we learned as we went, accompanied by Dr. Spock. Without him, none of us would have ever survived in those years!

The year that Enrique Jordá chose me as principal bassoonist, he chose Ross Taylor, who had been in the Cleveland Orchestra for three or four years, as principal horn player, and Phil Fath as principal clarinetist. They were the people who sat around me in the orchestra and they were all my age. Jordá knew how to build an orchestra and he built it damned well. But he was not a good technician and he was not a good conductor. He had a very warm sense of what the music was about—too warm. It went out from hand to foot and from foot to I don't know where, but it wasn't in the music. It was a real strange dichotomy. I have heard of other conductors like that, but I certainly didn't play with any of them.

When Pierre Monteux retired in 1952, there were two men who wanted the job as conductor of the San Francisco Symphony. One was Enrique Jordá, the second was Victor de Sabata. Can you imagine? The San Francisco Symphony almost hired one of the greats. At de Sabata's audition he conducted some pieces and they say that it was so exciting that men walked out of the hall with their hair standing straight up. But he conducted mostly opera, and that was one of the problems; he just didn't have the orchestral repertoire that was thought necessary to conduct a symphony orchestra. He could have learned the repertoire, but he didn't bother, because he preferred to conduct opera.

Jordá was an intelligent person, but he had some real hangups with religion. He was a good Roman Catholic. Whenever he had to go to a mass on Sunday and he would come to rehearsal afterwards, he would talk and talk for 53 minutes out of every hour, a compulsive kind of talking. The other seven minutes, we played. Concerts that were rehearsed on the weekends were not so good, because Jorda took so much of this as talking time and what musicians need to know when they prepare for a concert—above everything else—is to know the routine of the concert.

Jordá built the orchestra with seven of us who came in as principal players, but the orchestra still didn't sound good under him. Change of personnel happens with every new conductor. The first year a conductor takes over an orchestra it is always the honeymoon. The second year the new maestro has already picked the people he wants to fire. I don't know the percentages, but I do know that in the second year all hell breaks loose. No matter what we have written in the contract, it still happens. The damndest thing.

You could say that Jordá allowed the orchestra to deteriorate, but it wasn't a matter of "allowing" it to do anything. It's just that whoever is the taskmaster must have the discipline, attention, and knowledge required to make a good performance. And certainly Jordá didn't have it. He was there for seven years. It was a long time. Someone said he couldn't conduct his way out of a paper bag. He just was an awful conductor. But he was a lovely guy personally, and he had made me Principal Bassoonist of the San Francisco Symphony. I loved Jordá simply because I thought he was a real gentleman. He just couldn't conduct. Well, the next guy might be worse. You never know.

But the next guy was George Szell, who turned out to be an excellent musician, a learned man. He was a very crucial guest conductor. Szell was so good, it's what ended Jorda's career with the San Francisco Symphony. The critics started fighting with each other as to who was the best, Szell or Jordá. Szell wasn't there as a prospective permanent conductor, he was just there to conduct. Then he started telling people how rotten the orchestra was. The orchestra didn't like it. We had lost our morale. We wanted to defend what we had. That didn't work either. You finally have to be honest and say, "It's not working." If Jordá talked for 57 minutes and we could only rehearse for three minutes out of every hour, we really needed to get rid of the man because he wasn't doing anyone any good.

When Szell did a performance with the orchestra, it sounded good. But it was difficult to like him if you played under him. Very precise! Once, however, during the Tchaikovsky *Fourth Symphony,* as I faded the bassoon solo in the second movement, Szell gave me a big smile. That praise felt really good.

Let me tell you what the orchestra personnel thought about building an orchestra. We thought that the phrase "building an orchestra" was used for getting rid of a lot of very fine musicians. Did we feel that management needed an excuse for firing people? Absolutely. The European orchestras were great because they supported each and every player to the fullest. Even Szell was asked to restrict his vitriolic comments about the musicians in the European orchestras.

So when Szell came, the orchestra was the dregs. He told Alfred Frankenstein, the music critic of the *San Francisco Chronicle*, that it was the worst orchestra he'd ever heard and Frankenstein put it in the paper. And that started the whole thing going. That put Jordá's job on the line—more than on the line. His job was finished.

The years with Enrique Jordá in San Francisco were such that very few recordings were made. Jordá conducted recordings we made of the Prokofiev *Piano Concerto No. 3* with Gary Graffman and the Rachmaninoff *Piano Concerto No. 2* with Alexander Brailowsky, but what I remember vividly is the one we made of De Falla's *Nights in the Garden of Spain* with Artur Rubenstein. He was thrilling to work with. I still have a recording of that session from 1957. When we made a recording, we went into the hall, sat down, took out the music, and did Take Number One. There is a little green light and a little red light. When the green light goes on, you start playing, when the red light goes on you stop playing, The people in the booth backstage have their criticisms to make or you blew a note or something and you have a criticism to make. You want to be as exact as possible. If you make a mistake you certainly know. Everybody is totally honest in a recording. They may not be great, but they're honest, because there is so much technical equipment, especially now, with microphones that pick up everything.

In the recording session with Rubenstein he left a note out of one trill. The directors in the booth asked us to play it again. We did it five times. The fifth time was good, and they said "That is all we need." They spliced it right in.

In the old days it took quite a while for the technicians to set the balances correctly. They weren't as fussy as we are now and the recording equipment was much more difficult to bring into focus. Now they can do anything while making recordings, and they do! In some of the Mahler recordings with the San Francisco Symphony they spliced in the applause or if there was a cough or something disturbing they would splice it out. It's a wonderful thing. You can't tell. You don't know, unless you happen to be a musician. Now you do what you can to make sure that 32 violins play together and that you did your part correctly during every conscious moment.

When Rubenstein played he was a big deal in every respect. He was one of the greats, one of the best. Wonderful, so bravura. We played with him many times and he always had the same routine. He came onstage dressed like he was going to give a public address. Even for the first rehearsal, everything was in order, including a pearl stickpin in his tie. There would be a chair next to the piano and he would take his coat off and drape it carefully over the chair. Then he'd sit down, pull up his pants legs, and we'd play the damned piece through from beginning to end without stopping. Rubenstein was fascinating—an incredible man and a wonderful pianist. I wish we still had great artists and great personalities all wrapped up in one as we did in the time of Rubenstein.

After Enrique Jordá left San Francisco in 1963, I didn't see him again until 1972, when he attended a concert in Brussels where the orchestra was playing during our world tour. I couldn't talk to him that night because backstage was crowded. The next morning, while I was eating breakfast in the hotel dining room, I was called to the telephone. "This is Enrique Jordá, Mr. Green. I never had a chance to talk with you last night, so I thought I would give you a call." I said, "That is so nice of you, Maestro." Next he asked, "How is Mrs. Green?" "Just fine," I answered. Then Jordá said, "How are Nancy, David, and Peter?" This was like fifteen years later, and he remembered my kids. I was really impressed.

SAN FRANCISCO SYMPHONY
Enrique Jordá, Conductor and Musical Director

SIR THOMAS BEECHAM, *Guest Conductor*
February 10, February 11, February 12, 1960
War Memorial Opera House

Enrique
Jordá

SAN FRANCISCO SYMPHONY
Enrique Jordá, Conductor and Musical Director

Sir John Barbirolli, *Guest Conductor*
February 18, February 19, February 20, 1959
War Memorial Opera House

51ST Annual Season
SAN FRANCISCO SYMPHONY ORCHESTRA

ENRIQUE JORDÁ
conductor and
musical director

19 WEDNESDAYS
(FORUM CONCERTS)
at 8:30 P.M.

19 THURSDAYS
at 8:30 P.M.

19 FRIDAYS
at 2:15 P.M.

GUEST ARTISTS

Guest Conductors
JOSEF KRIPS
HOWARD MITCHELL
HANS SCHMIDT-ISSERSTEDT

Pianists
GEZA ANDA
CLAUDIO ARRAU
ALEXANDER BRAILOWSKY
LYA de BARBERIIS
PHILIPPE ENTREMONT
MALCOLM FRAGER
GLENN GOULD
HIRO IMAMURA
JOSE ITURBI

Violinists
CHRISTIAN FERRAS
TOSSY SPIVAKOVSKY

Guitarist
ANDRES SEGOVIA

CHORAL WORKS

DEBUSSY'S "THE BLESSED DAMOZEL"
DOROTHY WARENSKJOLD
MARGOT BLUM

HANDEL'S "MESSIAH"
LOIS MARSHALL
KATHERINE HILGENBERG
RAYMOND MANTON
DONALD GRAMM

BEETHOVEN'S "MISSA SOLEMNIS"
PHYLLIS CURTIN
CAROL SMITH
PAULINO SAHARREA
YI-KWEI SZE

MANAGED, MAINTAINED & PRESENTED BY THE SAN FRANCISCO SYMPHONY ASSOCIATION

J. D. ZELLERBACH, President
HOWARD K. SKINNER, Manager

SAN FRANCISCO SYMPHONY
Golden Season
Enrique Jordá, Conductor and Musical Director

MONTEUX, *Guest Conductor*
January 31, February 1, February 2, 1962
War Memorial Opera House

My first year in the Symphony we did some recording with Pierre Monteux when he was a guest conductor, just there for the recordings and some concerts that we played. Monteux was in his eighties, and just the most fabulous conductor. Papa Monteux. His musicianship was as solid as a rock. He was very gentle with his orchestra, who absolutely adored him. He had the most beautiful beat that I know of, none more beautiful, none more clear. Whenever I was waiting for an entrance cue—and I had about 20 measures to count rests, because there was nothing for me to do until my entrance—Monteux would look at me about a measure before and that big thick mustache would wiggle. And there was no way in the world that you would be left hanging or not understand what he wanted. And he knew just when and how to do it and how loud the click-click from smacking his lips would be. It was so hilarious, so marvelous! The audience couldn't hear it, but you could hear it. He was a just a great musician and cuing members of the orchestra was his great forte.

Monteux had a marvelous sense of humor. When he conducted the first performance of *The Rite of Spring*, in the middle of the performance the concertmaster tugged at Monteux's sleeve and said, "Pierre, Pierre, where are we?" Monteux answered, "Why do you ask me? Am I a prophet?" Mrs. Monteux had a dog by the name of FiFi that she brought to the rehearsals. That in itself was funny.

He could take pieces like Stravinsky's *The Rite of Spring* and *The Firebird* and *Petrouchka* and melt them into great original performances. He made many recordings with the San Francisco Symphony and man for man he was a giant, because he could take music and make it flow easily. He was truly one of the great conductors of the twentieth century. The orchestra gave Monteux a party at the Top of the Mark. We had an absolutely wonderful evening. It was a time I will never forget.

The San Francisco Opera

Some members of the San Francisco Symphony were also asked to play in the San Francisco Opera orchestra. When I started playing in the Opera, there was no audition. Kurt Herbert Adler, the general manager, was a wise bird. He heard me play in the Symphony. Could you hear a better audition? The one thing that you have to be careful of when you play in an opera, rather than in the symphony, is that you have no idea what an opera is about. You have no idea who's going to take what tempo, who's going to walk across the stage faster than they did the last time in the rehearsal. I figure it takes about four years to earn your keep.

I was under contract to the San Francisco Symphony and the San Francisco Opera. I was one of the musicians lucky enough to play the opera. Opera is totally different. You forget everything you know. All people who hadn't played opera before found that out. What happens then is that you learn to play opera and you learn to play symphonies and you get to be in a very wonderful orchestra because of this flexibility and malleability and everything in between. The chorus may be doing something wild, weird, that shouldn't be done at all and they do it and you follow along meekly. If you don't know it, you get lost! The thing is, you have solo singers, solo performers, choral performers, dance, and scenery changes, all going on, sometimes at once.

I remember walking into the opera for the first time and there was my friend, Eric Leinsdorf, about to conduct a performance of the Strauss Der Rosenkavalier. I had played under him in Rochester, but I never played Rosenkavalier and I want to tell you, that's one of the hardest, if not the hardest opera ever written. That is a tough mother! It really is. All the Strauss operas are. The orchestration and this incredible tension and attention are the two things that you need in the Strauss opera. Let's say you are playing a

Backstage with the San Francisco Opera Orchestra, 1958

Mozart opera or a Wagner opera and you momentarily get lost in a performance. You look at the second bassoon and most likely he has troubles also, but you can find your way. With Strauss, you have to pay attention, because if you're lost, you are never going to find your way back. It's even true in *Rosenkavalier*, especially in the third act. It's a very beautiful opera, just marvelous. *Ariadne auf Naxos* has a fourteen piece orchestra and that's it. It is very lightly orchestrated Strauss, which is unheard of in opera. What Strauss thought about the trumpets is they should be seen and not heard. He was actually quoted as saying that.

The orchestration in *Rosenkavalier* is difficult and also what you're asked to do is difficult. What happens is that you are going great in the first act and somehow, in the middle, you lose your place, because it's long and it's constant, and you have to watch the singers: *dee deee da da dum*. Well, it's not written that way. It should be: *da de de da da da daaa*. You know why I held that note? It's not there, but that is a tradition that's been incorporated into all performances by everybody. So, you're sitting there and you're sweating and wondering where you are. You have to ask the second bassoonist, "Where are we?" That's really pretty awful. And it gets worse as you go on and you get into the second act and you think, "He wouldn't dare, would he?" Yes, he would. And you can't learn those things by just having the music. You need to be well versed in the tradition and tradition is everything in opera.

I sat down and I trembled and I sort of made it through *Rosenkavalier* and Maestro Leinsdorf yelled at me, then he subdivided a little spot in such a way that I couldn't make heads or tails of it. He was conducting everything from memory, of course. He had put the score on the side somewhere. Never looked at it, even for rehearsals. He was such an egomaniac, you wouldn't believe it. Leinsdorf gave nothing to the musicians and was a man who carried grudges. He got so mad at one performer in the first act of *Der Rosenkavalier* that he knocked over the music stand of the principal flutist, which made a big dent in his silver flute. We had to call the union president to come down, who told Leinsdorf the performance would not go on until he apologized to the whole orchestra. It got that bad. And worse!

At one point, Leinsdorf said, "No, no, bassoon . . . " I still couldn't get it. He said, "Come see me in my dressing room." So I went up and he had written the part out very clearly, on a piece of paper. It wasn't even music paper. He just drew the lines and wrote it out and at the bottom he wrote, "With my best regards to Walter Green." And I got it. I never missed that spot again. When I arrived outside after the next rehearsal, Maestro Leinsdorf came by and said, "Have some peanuts, Mr. Green." I thanked him profusely.

At the end of the first season, we were just ready to leave the pit when Leinsdorf looked over at me and at our principal clarinetist, Phil Fath, and said, "Mr. Green. Mr. Fath.

When you play together and you play in tune, you sound very well!" He had an Oxford accent, with German mixed in, which is a weird combination. That's all he said.

Our assistant principal trumpet player was kind of a square and he asked Leinsdorf what was written for the second trumpet in the "penultimate" measure. When the orchestra heard "penultimate" they let out an "Oh, yeah." Leinsdorf said, "Why are you making this fuss? This man speaks good English."

Leinsdorf was on the verge of being great, except he was an egomaniac, and cold. My teacher in Vienna, Karl Ohlberger, once asked me if I had ever heard of a man named Erich Landauer, who would supposedly become a great conductor. I didn't hear about Leinsdorf until I got to Rochester. I understand that he left Vienna because he was Jewish and went to New York and started out conducting Wagner's *Ring of the Nibelungen* from memory at the Metropolitan Opera—every note! I talked to people who played with him. He had changed his name. Doesn't make sense, but there we are. Leinsdorf had an ego like you wouldn't believe.

A rheostat was used in Poulenc's *Dialogues of the Carmelites*, to make the pit go light and dark, and Leinsdorf had to take care of it. He needed it to come in at certain times with the orchestra. When he pushed the rheostat down, he would make a distasteful face.

One night after a performance of *Rosenkavalier*, he walked past the pit and I heard him say to conductor William Steinberg, in German, "There are so many notes being dropped, we could write another opera from them." Leinsdorf and Steinberg were friends. They both came from Germany and both were Jewish. Leinsdorf was good, but he just didn't have much warmth. Steinberg was warmer than Leinsdorf. Both were excellent musicians and when attending one of their performance one usually heard good solid music-making.

When William Steinberg was close to death, they put a cot in the studio so he could rest during intermissions. We were rehearsing the Beethoven *Seventh* with the Symphony. Steinberg put his baton down halfway through the rehearsal and said, "Ladies and Gentlemen, you've played this at least as often as I have. Let's just play it tonight." And the orchestra played the Beethoven *Seventh* like you never heard it. He was dead ten days later. We all grieved for the loss of this great conductor.

The conductor Karl Boehm was really one of the "biggies" and we played with him for one year. We were doing the Strauss *Die Frau Ohne Schatten* and I came down with the flu so bad that my temperature jumped up to 104°. They flew in the principal bassoonist of the Metropolitan Opera to take my place. I came back after the first two performances. There's a huge five-minute bassoon solo, with nothing else playing except the bassoon, in the third act. Boehm was conducting. Up came my solo and I played solo beautifully. When I finished I thought I'd get a nice smile from him, or something, but all he gave me was the shortest look known to man. His look of approval must have been at least one-tenth of second long. That was it. That was a "Thank you, you sounded great!" Such a short thank-you was all you would get from him. Bohem looked like the super Nazi that he was, but he was really good with Strauss operas. He was, I think, extremely antisocial.

We had a good French conductor named Georges Prêtre. He's made a lot of recordings. We did Wagner's *Parsifal* with him, which is almost six hours. It's unbelievable what goes on and it's truly beautiful music. He also conducted Bizet's *Carmen* and Debussy's *Pelléas et Mélisande* with us. Prêtre perspired heavily, to such a degree that half the orchestra would be dripping wet during performances. But he was very good.

We also played *Pelléas et Mélisande* with Jean Martinon, who was never popular with audiences, but who was a superb conductor, very interesting. We were lucky to have him. He had us play so softly that the woodwinds were sucking instead of blowing. You can do that, but it takes a hell of a lot of control. Every time I put my bassoon to my mouth and would play he would "Shhhhhhhh!" Even in concerts, it would happen. But he knew that opera inside out and it made sense to me for the first time. If you listen to a recording of it, and only turn the volume up half way, you might like it. I didn't ever like that opera before, but I did after playing it with Martinon. But I've never seen it, sitting in an audience; I've only played it. In the pit you don't see much, especially in an opera like *Pelléas et Mélisande*, where there is very little movement. Martinon was once principal conductor of the Chicago Symphony, but he was fired and nobody knows why.

The French conductors were very good, like Charles Munch, who used to conduct the Boston Symphony and made lots of good recordings. He conducted us when we did the Dutilleux *Concerto for Four Solo Wind Instruments with Orchestra*. I loved playing that with Munch and I thought he was great.

Another favorite conductor of mine was the little-known Leopold Ludwig. I played with him a lot, in opera. He had the greatest way of starting Strauss's *Die Frau Ohne Schatten*, as if he was possessed. And he was a nice man. He was the conductor of the Hamburg Opera.

One of the three or four greatest conductors that no-body knew was Francesco Molinari-Pradelli, a secondary conductor at the Metropolitan Opera. He was interested in me and used to take me out to dinner after the performance. He conducted mostly opera, but I played one symphonic concert with him. All I can say is that he was like what the young Toscanini must have been. When Molinari-Pradelli would give a downbeat, it was like fire coming out of the note. He did the Verdi operas better than anyone else I've heard. We did the last two Verdi operas, *Otello* and *Falstaff*, and I never knew how great these operas were until I played with Molinari-Pradelli. Marvelous conductor.

There were a lot of very wonderful conductors who got their start in opera. Toscanini was essentially an opera conductor, and so was Bruno Walter.

Kurt Herbert Adler did conduct, but he wasn't very good. When he conducted we used to say, "He is changing the kitty litter." He knew everything about opera, but he had a hard time making his body move in conductorial movements, so as a conductor he was awkward. He knew everything about every piece of music that he ever had anything to do with. And he was an amazingly great impresario. He just couldn't conduct.

Adler was into everything. He told you what time it was, when to get up, when to go to bed, when to have sex with your wife, when to have sex without your wife. He knew it and he would tell you.

My bassoons were destroyed when our house burned down, and I didn't have a bassoon to play. I heard about a visiting bassoonist who had a Heckel for sale. I called this guy, who was a famous bassoonist, and asked him if he would sell the bassoon to me. "How much is it?" He said, "$2400." I said, "Sold!" But I couldn't pick up that bassoon in Berkeley until the next day, so meanwhile I used an old instrument given to me by a friend.

At that night's performance we were doing Verdi's *Aida*. There's an *obligato* to the soprano halfway though the second act. The soprano was the wonderful Leontyne Price. Adler came down to the pit afterwards and curled his nose, like he'd never heard anything so bad. I said, "What's the matter, Maestro?" He said, "Zat is not your regular instrument, is it?" I said, "No, it isn't." He said, "See that you get one." I already had it in my hind pocket. I brought the new bassoon in the next day. We came to that spot in the music and at the end of the rehearsal Adler came running down the aisle of the opera house saying, "Yes, yes!" He was that good.

Adler was the harshest critic that I've ever seen. I don't mean that he was a critic, but he wanted to run everything. He was the captain of the ship, or the general. You could never quite get mad at him, because he was such a curmudgeon. He was also a gentleman every once in a while, if the mood struck him—but it didn't strike very often. He knew opera better than anyone I've ever known, but the orchestra never quite admitted that. I was certainly not of that opinion then, because Adler was sparing in his praise. Things would get to a point where we were begging for compliments.

I remember Gelando Josie, who was the principal trombonist of the orchestra under Monteux and Jorda. Adler came out of the pit one day, walked past me, gave me a glare, and walked on. Josie said to Adler, "How was that, Maestro. How was that?" Adler answered, "TERRIBLE!" That's the way it went. Even if it was good, it was never good enough. Which is the way it should be, I think. With art, there's always something more that one can do or bring in that makes it better. But if you don't pay attention and you're not devoted to your art, then it isn't going to happen. There's nothing so bad for an orchestra as complacency.

It's like anything else, you know. People are in a quandary when they can't get something to happen, so they use anger and force. That doesn't work. But they never learn that. Fritz Reiner never learned it, yet, as a conductor, he was as good as they come. He guest conducted the Symphony and he conducted the Opera, and we wanted to kill him. We were playing *Salome* by Richard Strauss, which Reiner was famous for conducting. It is another of those crazy, difficult operas by Richard Strauss. There is only one act, but it is hard to stay focused on what you are doing, because it is so damned difficult. It was the same with *Electra* and the same with *Die Frau Ohne Schatten*. I don't know which is the hardest to perform.

Reiner had a face like Dracula. He was the world's meanest conductor, but he was a great conductor. He had an amazing control of the orchestra, because the beat was so small, so infinitesimal, that if you looked away for just one second you'd be lost. When you looked at his baton you were completely mesmerized. The baton said everything that it needed to say, but it was horrendous. He was an evil man in the way he treated musicians and his colleagues, probably worse than any other conductor. He first had the Pittsburgh Symphony, then the Chicago Symphony. When he was in the Chicago orchestra the guys were all sick. They had stomach ailments and such because of the way he treated them. But he did wonderful recordings there. He was the best Strauss conductor, except for Richard Strauss himself. Strauss would stand and conduct with no expression in the face at all. None whatsoever. And every once in a while during a performance he'd take out his watch and look to see what time it was!

We had a bass clarinetist, Mr. Frugale, who, because of his age, was in the last weeks of his career. During rehearsal of *Salome* he made a mistake of some kind. I don't know what, because I was too busy learning my own part to fuss with him. Reiner said, "Mr. Frugale, do you know ver we arrrrre?" Frugale looked up at him and, since this was his last rehearsal, the clarinetist answered, "No, are you lost too, Maestro?" One of the great stories of the Opera.

One time we were going to perform Beethoven's *Fidelio* and at the last moment Adler let the orchestra know that his two guests that evening were Lotte Lehman and Bruno Walter—and Walter was conducting! He had conducted both Lehman and *Fidelio* 1500 times. Well, that orchestra responded in excitement in a way that is unmatched to

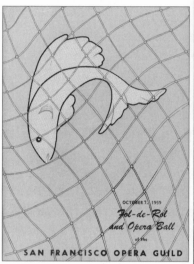

OCTOBER 7, 1959
Fol-de-Rol
and Opera Ball
of the
SAN FRANCISCO OPERA GUILD

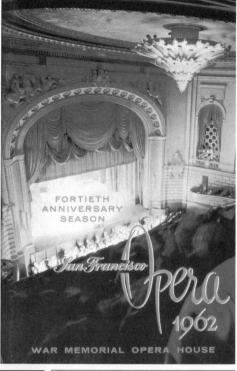

FORTIETH
ANNIVERSARY
SEASON

San Francisco
Opera
1962

WAR MEMORIAL OPERA HOUSE

PERFORMING ARTS

1970

SanFranciscoOpera

SAN FRANCISCO OPERA

KURT HERBERT ADLER
General Director

HOWARD K. SKINNER
Manager

TWO EXTRA PERFORMANCES

Monday, October 22, at 8:30 p.m.

LA BOHEME

De Los Angeles, Horne; Cioni, Tipton, Christopher,
Macurdy, Baccaloni, Fried, Harvey, Andersen

Conductor: Molinari-Pradelli   *Staged by:* Yannopoulos

Designer: Jenkins

Wednesday, October 24, at 8:00 p.m.

I PAGLIACCI

Lipp; Del Monaco, Bastianini, Christopher,
Manton, Riffel, Drain

followed by

CAVALLERIA RUSTICANA

Simionato, Martin, Cole; Sullivan, Tipton

Conductor: De Fabritiis   *Staged by:* Capobianco

TICKETS AVAILABLE: Opera-Symphony Box Office, Sherman Clay &
Co., Kearny and Sutter St., EX 7-0717 and
all Bay Area agencies.

SanFranciscoOpera

48th Annual Season

September 18 to November 29

War Memorial Opera House

Kurt Herbert Adler
GENERAL DIRECTOR

Die Frau
ohne Schatten

San
Francisco
Opera

Kurt Herbert Adler, general director

54th Season
September 10 through November 28, 1976
War Memorial Opera House

PERFORMING ARTS

SanFranciscoOpera
1972
FiftiethSeason

113

this day. It was a marvelous, wonderful performance. This kind of thing made me love opera.

Sometimes you do a separate orchestral rehearsal, without the singers. Sometimes you take an old war horse like Puccini's *La Bohème*, where the first act is 13 minutes, the second act is 17 minutes, and so on. But you have no idea of what's going to happen, regardless of how much you have rehearsed. This walking across the stage is a good example of things. It's not that we can't do other things also, but when one of the artists walks across the stage, everyone has to pay attention. The conductor has to slow down or speed up the orchestra, depending on how strong the conductor is. I remember one instance when William Steinberg sat with his hand on his chin during a performance of Mussorgsky's *Boris Godouov* when the bass singing Boris took a little different tempo than he had in the rehearsals. Steinberg, who had a fat head, wouldn't change his tempo. "Either my way or nothing!" So it was a bad performance of *Boris*.

These kinds of shenanigans happened more than once during those years when I was playing with the Opera company. Steinberg conducted everything from memory. I remember we did Verdi's *A Masked Ball*. It was a bad performance because Steinberg couldn't get along with the soprano. There is no one quite as stupid as a soprano, except maybe a tenor. But this ingredient can make things very interesting, because you never let go of anything that you have in your bag of tricks, just because somebody is dragging the performance. There isn't a musician in a million who would do anything destructive on purpose.

The conductor can speed up a singer during a performance by increasing the tempo of the music so the singer has some choice, but then a game starts between the tenor and the soprano. I remember a wonderful example of this during a performance of Donizetti's *Lucia di Lammamoor*. If you are a musician you are pulled into a million pieces trying to follow everyone at the same time. These are traps that are removable with good, sensitive musicianship.

I also remember when Luciano Pavarotti sang with this wonderful Spanish soprano, a big fat mama whose name I've forgotten, in Puccini's *Tosca*. They ignored the conductor from beginning to end but they were so big, as singers, that Adler swallowed his pride and let them get away with it.

With the San Francisco Opera there was only one soloist in *Otello*. Placido Domingo. I played with him almost every year. Whenever he was finished with a performance, he would take out his handkerchief, and wave tenderly to his audience before he bowed. Beverly Sills sang opposite him a few times. It's unfortunate those two magicians never made recordings together.

All of us fell in love with Sills. She was a dear, dear person. I remember once doing a performance of Donizetti's *Lucia di Lammermoor* with the big Mad Scene. We were rehearsing and Sills came onstage and dove right into the Mad Scene and did it without stopping. I mean she didn't stop for anything. I found out that three and a half weeks before she'd had a cancer operation. She was a real trouper. She used to sing in the San Francisco Opera Chorus when she was still a teenager. Now she occasionally comes out of semi-retirement, on television, but the voice isn't there any more; it's gone.

It's like Lily Pons, who came in one day to raise funds. She hadn't sung for years and the middle and bottom of her voice were just about gone, but the top was still there. The top was still there! We couldn't believe it, and we couldn't believe that Adler got her to come sing with us.

Then there was Maria Callas, who had an imperfect voice, but she made magic more times than anyone I knew of as a singer. Her singing was super phenomenal. But she didn't sing in tune some of the time, and that really bothered the hell out of me.

There wasn't much the conductor could do with the big-time stars. He had nothing to say. With them, opera conductors just did their bidding.

I had the good fortune to play with some great singers, like Placido Domingo, Leontyne Price, Robert Merrill, Victoria de los Angeles, and Beverly Sills. And the truly most wonderful part of playing for the opera was that you got a chance to rub elbows or noses or whatever with these great artists. Orchestra members could have any kind of rapport with the artists that they wanted. And it was wonderful to hear somebody pull a beautiful phrase, which is something that no one except a professional musician would even understand. Somebody would sing something so divinely beautiful that you wanted to drop your instrument and start crying. Sitting there and playing with these great, great artists was a joy.

I remember one incident with this very big, fat soprano. We were doing a performance with her, out of town. My father was with me. I put him in a chair backstage and let him watch from that angle. There was a circular stairway that came down backstage. An elderly dowager started falling down the stairway and this soprano caught her and said, "Holy shit, lady! I thought you'd fall on your fucking ass!" My father looked at me in amazement.

For me, without misunderstanding, I must say that I enjoyed playing opera more than symphony concerts because of all of those extras that came with it. Once you knew your way, Adler could come and say, "We're having a performance of *La Bohème* tonight with so and so." This was like my fourth opera, and there was no rehearsal, nothing. I didn't know shit from Shinola. We played the performance and it was letter perfect. I was ten pounds lighter, which is okay. This is the kind of thing that would happen.

That had to be repertoire stuff. Then every third or fourth year you played something like Puccini's *Il Tabarro* or *Gianni*

Schicchi, and you had to sight read the music, quickly. And then came a Janacek opera, which you couldn't read, period—and the first performance was pretty shaky! Beautiful operas, though, wonderful stuff.

With the symphony, it was a 10:00 a.m. call, you had a 10:00 to 1:00 rehearsal, and that was that. Then you played three or four concerts of the music that you had rehearsed. Once in a great while there would be music you had played three weeks before, which some rich society woman wanted to hear again, so they squeezed it in somewhere, but that was an exception. With the opera that wasn't so much of an exception. It's something that happened frequently.

The love of playing in an opera orchestra is difficult to explain if you haven't sat in the pit. You're playing music. A lot is going on. You have to be aware of what's happening, but you've still got to concentrate mostly on playing. But the little amount that I received from the actual performance was enough to make me feel like I did as a young man, when I listened to all those 78 rpm recordings, which I really loved and bought with care, and cherished, whoever was playing or conducting.

It was that difference between the symphony and the opera, and at the end of the opera season we'd be so wiped out, so dead tired, that we didn't know how we could start a symphony season the next week. There was never any time for anything in the opera and also, to a degree, in the symphony. You never had enough rehearsal. Your white tie was wearing out. Whatever it was, there was never enough time. When you played principal in the opera, you had better know what you are doing. All I know is that what I learned in opera performance was more than I learned in symphony performance and solo performances—ten times as much!

I loved the opera and I loved performing the opera, but we sat in misery downstairs. Sometimes the pit was so small, simply because the orchestra was so large, that you would just sit there and sweat all evening because the atmosphere was lacking in ozone or something. Adler was going to fix that. He put some special material, a scrim, over the pit and then the loudness was just right for Adler. We were softer than ever, but the temperature got up to 85°, 89°. We had little fans on our music stands. Then we called the union in and they made them tear those scrims off. I understand that since they remodeled the opera house that's all been changed and the musicians now have good places to sit. Back then it was a pretty raw place, physically.

After we were through with the San Francisco Opera season, we used to play ten days of opera performances in Los Angeles. The whole orchestra and the whole cast would go down in a night train. We sat in front of the pool all day and played at night. It was a wonderful life. I loved the opera. After a while, I knew it inside out. I really knew it. That made all the difference.

〄

After Enrique Jordá left, they picked Josef Krips as the new conductor and Krips was going to make the San Francisco Symphony into the Vienna Philharmonic. Krips was trained as a Vienna Choir Boy and had a long musical career, having trained under one of the great European conductors, Felix Weingartner. Krips was resident conductor of the Vienna Staatsoper and a professor at the Vienna Academy until the Nazis annexed Austria in 1938. After the war he conducted many orchestras, including the Vienna State Opera and the Vienna Philharmonic. In 1946 he reopened the Salzburg Festival. Before Krips came to San Francisco, he was the conductor of the Buffalo Philharmonic. He was our permanent conductor through 1970. He had become a major conductor, and he did a really superb job conducting operas.

Krips had a reputation as a benevolent despot, and living in San Francisco didn't lighten him up. He would click his heels and say, "No boots in this orchestra! This is not the Gold Rush days." He was, so to speak, allowed to click *his* boots, but no one else in the orchestra could do it. Krips had a saying for each occasion. "Don't play crudely. This is not the '49ers. Play like the Vienna Philharmonic."

Krips might have been grateful, but it wasn't in his nature. I helped de-Nazify the Vienna Philharmonic while I was in Vienna, and after the war Krips was given the job as the conductor of the Vienna Philharmonic because he was politically a zero. He was absolutely clean. Krips was not Jewish, but evidently his grandmother was, so therefore, to the Nazis, his mother was, and if his mother was, that meant he was Jewish. Actually, he was raised Catholic, but to the Nazis he was "persona non grata." His mother or grandmother had worked in a pickle factory during the war, so we always said of Krips, "He's working in a pickle factory today."

What we found out, though, was very interesting. Whenever Krips had the baton in his hand, when he was conducting, it was always the tempo of his heartbeat. We didn't know what his heartbeat was, but we surmised. It went bunk, bunk, bunk, ta da dump tia da dee. That's the Mozart *G Minor Symphony*. Mostly it was good. Anything transferred from 4/4 to 2/4. If it's in 3, it could be in 1. He almost plodded, but he didn't. I was at the concert in Vienna when Herbert Von Karajan was permitted to conduct again after the war, and the difference in tempos between Krips and Von Karajan with that same orchestra was astounding. Von Karajan was a young man then and very exciting. Regardless of his political affiliations, he was undoubtedly a great conductor.

During his tenure in San Francisco Krips started many arguments with members of the orchestra. In one dress rehearsal Maestro Krips was upset with the chorus rehearsing for the Beethoven *Ninth Symphony* and he said, "I have only two things to say to you, im-possible!"

Krips once insulted one of the women in the orchestra, telling her that she wasn't good enough. He was just terrible to her. He read her out backstage, but in front of other members of the orchestra. It was one of those things that happen occasionally in orchestras, when a conductor yells at a player. She was just getting her fiddle out to start the rehearsal. He started in on her, how rotten she played, out of tune and no sense of rhythm—every insult he could think of, and he didn't couch it in a nice way. The orchestra decided that we wouldn't let this go by. We went to see Krips and told him that if he didn't correct this in some way, we would not play for him any more.

So the old man decided to apologize to the orchestra and it was a classic psychological scene. Krips got up in front of the orchestra and said, "Ven a Father scolds his children, zat does not mean he does not love zem." That's word for word. It's been in my memory for a long time. That happened about four years into his tenure.

I have a personal ax to grind with Mr. Krips. I personally do not think he deserves much praise. I had a memory lapse in a rhythm that was written in the second movement of the Brahms *Fourth Symphony*. I thought, "What did I do wrong?" The music was printed wrong, a printing error. I just goofed because I missed it. It was one of my seven goofs. It's not unusual for there to be printing errors. There are lots of them. That's why the big deal comes about how to keep to the intentions of the composer. Well, you can't really do it, because there are too many printing errors—first in the manuscript, then the transfer, then the final printed score.

This was during a rehearsal on a Saturday morning. Krips became so angry at me that he jumped off the podium and spit in my face. Who knows why he got so upset about my mistake? Krips rarely used a score, certainly not with the major symphonies by Mozart, Beethoven, or Brahms, so he might not have been aware of the printing errors. Or he might not have cared and was angry at me anyway because I had studied with his fair-haired boy at the Vienna Philharmonic. My teacher, Karl Ohlberger, had been his first bassoonist in the Vienna Philharmonic after the war, and I had studied with Burghauser in New York, whom Krips also knew. Big deal! When he came to San Francisco, he remembered all of that. But that was enough to set him off. I just stayed away from him. I knew enough by then to stay as far away from conductors as I could.

Once when I had a terrible bladder infection I went into his room to ask him to have an extra bassoonist there just in case I couldn't keep playing. You know what his answer was? He pointed to my shoe. "Tie your shoe lace." Nothing else. That's what his response was. I was suffering, yet he wouldn't recognize that.

We were playing in Pittsburg, California and the program was Beethoven's *Third Leonore Overture*, the *Sixth Symphony*, and the *Fifth Symphony*. Well, Krips, in his idiotic head, decided that we were playing the *Third Leonore Overture*, the Beethoven *Fifth*, and then the Beethoven *Sixth*. And he gave a downbeat . . . *whishh, da da to dee da pa* . . . We went absolutely crazy. He was conducting the wrong work on the program!

I got even with Krips a couple of times. We had a job outside of the symphony with pickup members of the orchestra and people from the outside playing with us on a Mozart Symphony. Not a festival, just an odd concert. Krips was conducting. I made one of my many mistakes and he said, "Wat was dat?" I said, "That's a mistake, sir," which was a funny enough retort to have gotten into the Hall of Fame of orchestra retorts. But not only that, Krips said,

"When I have to play the Mozart *39th Symphony*, I prepare for it for a whole month," and I said, "So do I, sir. So do I!" He grumbled about something. At intermission, I asked the personnel manager if I could go in to see Mr. Krips. He said, "Yeah, you can go in now." I asked, "Is there anyone with him?" He said, "No, absolutely not!" I asked him, "Are you sure this is an outside job?" He said, "Yes, I'm positive." I said, "Show me the contract." He showed me the contract and I knew I could do what I wanted to do. I knocked on Krips's door. He said, "Yah, come in." There he stood. He was naked from the waist up and he had a cigar in his mouth. I said, "Maestro, I just want you to know that you're just a son of a bitch and I'm going to hit you now." I ran after him. We ran around the conductor's room four or five times. Honest to God.

Things like this happened, and not only in San Francisco. George Szell was conducting the Cleveland Orchestra. The assistant concertmaster was Anschel Brusilov, who was one of the great orchestral violin players. One morning Szell insulted Brusilov in rehearsal quite a few times. Brusilov went into the Szell's room and said, "Maestro, if you ever talk to me like that again, I'm going to hit you. I'm going to kill you!" Szell's reply was, "Ach, Anschel. I love you when you're mad!" He made himself ridiculous in front of the whole orchestra. It happened all the time. All the time.

The conductor of the New Orleans Symphony was named Werner Torkanovsky. Our principal clarinetist, Philip Fath, said, "Maestro. Can you tell me . . ." Torkanovsky interrupted Phil and said, "Don't call me Maestro. Call me Werner!" Phil said, "Yeah. I wanted to call you something," and Torkanovsky said, "You're fired!" I've heard such horror stories about Serge Koussevitzky. His second clarinetist in the Boston Symphony, in those years, was Manny Volario. After Koussevitzky was buried, Volario went out to the grave and xxx'ed all over it. The clarinetist felt so abused that it drove him into a frenzy.

Sometimes a musician just couldn't resist responding to what was going on, even at his own peril. Our bassoon section changed around and I had a new second bassoonist who made the greatest faux pas in music of all time. We had an assistant conductor who was totally insignificant. We were rehearsing a children's concert with the San Francisco Symphony. It was so badly conducted that we could hardly keep still. This guy was conducting because his father owned a Swiss bank, and his conducting was just hideous. The second bassoonist raised his hand and said to the conductor, "Are my shoes ready yet?" I almost fell out of my seat. Needless to say, the second bassoonist did not survive the season.

But some players were above it. Paul Renzi, our principal flutist in San Francisco, never had an encounter with a conductor. We used to tease him, that he only made one mistake a year. We all made mistakes, but he less than anybody. We'd say, "Oh, that's it! That's enough for this time!" He was that good. His father had played principal oboe in the NBC Symphony. Paul played principal flute at age seventeen in the San Francisco Symphony. Then he went to the NBC Symphony, where he sat next to his father, who played first oboe. His grandfather was an organist at the Vatican. There are those musicians who come close to perfection. They play their best, no matter what, and they are of another class. Paul goes on and on. He loves to play baseball with the kids around the block, and when he doesn't play baseball, he sits at the piano and reduces operas, at sight, playing from beginning to end.

The Symphony made two overseas tours during my time with the orchestra. One of them was to Japan with Krips, on a chartered plane. When we were outside of Osaka, the plane's landing lights went on, but the airport landing lights did not. We swooped down and went into a steep ascent and we all thought it was over. The second time we went to the right of the first time and did the same kind of maneuver. The third time the plane came in right over the runway. Evidently, they had lost power in the airport tower. We were pretty frightened. Sitting next to me on the flight was a woman who had been a student of a great Czechoslovakian violin teacher. There are always these great violin teachers. When the plane came down so steeply then went back up again, this woman went panicky. I slapped her face and did all the things the movies tell you to do, and she stopped. I was more nervous than she was.

As we left the plane, Krips said, "Meet me in the elevator." I met him in the elevator. It was the only time on the trip that I saw him, except on the podium. "Remember," he said, "This is not a vacation." There I was after being on an airplane for 150 hours, it seemed like, and then he thought I was taking this trip as a vacation. It's the kind of thing that really made you feel, "Oh God! More of this!" It doesn't sound or mean that much when you take it by itself, but it really becomes tedious. Josef Krips was, to say the least, very strange.

The Working Musician

What no one ever talks about is that playing in a symphony orchestra is a job, but it's not like any other job. It's not like having a 40-hour-a-week job. Everybody who is professional regards this as a full-time job, but some people are more devoted than others. It just comes with the territory. There are some people who don't practice and just show up for the rehearsals and the performance and that's it. But they are exceptions.

There is constant pressure. There is always that level of tension, the player's anxiety, which began with me while I was at the Eastman School. And it was always there. The difficulty of a piece did not determine the amount of anxiety or how anxiety-ridden you were. It was just something that happened. The principal tympanist of the New York Philharmonic, Roland Koloff, played with us for some years, and at the appropriate moment he would whisper to me, "Floating anxieties, Walter, floating anxieties." That meant you couldn't really explain it. It was just there. I have tried, honest to God; I have tried everything in the world, including therapy and different religions. But I still couldn't rid myself of the anxiety. Pop the Inderal, and I could do it.

My good friend, Mark Lifshey, was principal oboist of the National Symphony in Washington, D.C., then he became principal oboe in the Cleveland Orchestra under George Szell, and finally, was principal oboist of the San Francisco Symphony. Each time you talked with Mark about music you ended up getting a lesson. Not that he was trying to teach you or anything, but the information that he had to give about music was so profound. He said, "I hate the oboe. I hate playing. I just don't like it. I just hate it." I said, "Mark, what are you saying?" "I don't want to play any more. It's just lousy. It's just anxiety-ridden." In fact, Mark never got anxious for a moment. Never. I never saw him shake or anything. The reason he didn't was that he was prepared. He played so beautifully, that we all learned from him every time he put his oboe to his mouth. He had played and played, ever since he was a boy. When he came to an age where one could fairly reasonably think about retirement, he still had a son to bring through college. He didn't ever dry up. He always played beautifully. But he hated music. I don't know how anyone can play that beautifully and hate music. He hated the music business. He hated the oboe. He hated making reeds. He just didn't like it. He quit the symphony and found a job at Indiana University as the oboe teacher and also chamber music instructor and that lasted another eight years.

We often played without enough practice time. I used to play both the Opera and the Symphony concerts. When we had to play the opera instead of the symphony, you went crazy because you didn't know the repertoire. It took about three or four years to learn all the operas well enough so that you could just go in and play at sight, which was often necessary. There was more work and more work and more work.

Now there are associate principals. They didn't have them for many years. Each principal player now plays half the concert. That gives the principal player a rest. If you're playing Wagner's *Ring*, you need two long intermissions in order to catch your breath. Phil Fath, our principal clarinetist, would look at me in the second half of an opera and whisper, "I can't make it any more!" "Me too, Phil, I know I can't." Then he'd say to me, "We'll go on." When you played *Die Meistersinger*, the first act is an hour and ten minutes long. The second act is an hour long and you think you are through with it but no, there is still the third act, which is an hour and forty-five minutes long. Do you know what you feel like after that? Mincemeat!!! It's just very, very strenuous work.

When I was in San Francisco, it was an average of 70 hours a week, with four rehearsals, four or five concerts, teaching at the conservatory, teaching at home, making reeds. Then you drop dead of fatigue. After 1968, we were under contract for 52 weeks of the year. The teaching was not part of the job, but it's an element in the way you live. You put it all together to have an income that you can live on. You've got three kids at home with Mama and that still puts more tension on you. Because it used to be, if you didn't do something well and right to begin with, you were in trouble with management and the conductor. The voice of orchestral musicians became stronger and stronger as the years wandered on. These younger players are so solid in their techniques that most likely they play with fewer anxieties than we ever did.

Do you think it was any different in Indianapolis? Absolutely not. The pressure there was for only 22 weeks, but afterwards there was no employment, which created other anxieties. The Vienna Philharmonic once did an experiment on how much tension was caused while playing a concert. They wired everybody in the orchestra up and took EEG readings. The results showed that playing in a symphony orchestra was one of the highest-tension jobs known to man. The next level higher is a brain surgeon.

Playing in the Vienna Philharmonic and many other European orchestras is, in fact, a little easier because they are government subsidized. In Vienna musicians don't even have to buy their own instruments. Imagine, a hall where during intermission the musicians can get something to drink or a sandwich or even have a martini.

When one is a bassoonist playing the last movement of Beethoven's *Fourth Symphony*, the level of tension is incredibly high and there is nobody there except you. If it doesn't go well at the first rehearsal, you're dead to begin with. We all have off days. What I used to do if I came into a concert and I was having a hard time, was purposely play a note that didn't belong in the music, to get it over with. I would be the only person to hear it and I could think, well, I'm not perfect or anything close to it, and that would be it. That worked. You've got to find out things like that. You've already played a wrong note. There won't be another one, at least not until the next time.

The anxieties are increased because of what seems to be a continual antagonism between the orchestra and the conductor. Which I don't think is necessary at all, but if you're going to go up and face a hundred men and women who have such knowledge as I've described throughout this book, they damn well better know what they are doing. And if they don't, they're going to get it. And certain conductors will give it back, and there are continual encounters.

The conductor is the boss, period. No matter how it seems, the conductor is the boss, but it is less so now, because the union contracts are getting stronger, so that the musicians don't get spit on and things like that. What I'm doing, instead of painting a heavenly picture, is to try to show you what was real in my years as a symphony player.

I want you to know that everything made up for the terrible tension that was present in orchestral playing. I mean that. It was 60 percent pleasure and 40 percent not, including 10 percent of real antagonism. It wasn't just a straight line. So I was amply rewarded for my struggles over the years. What kept us sane playing in symphony orchestras was that the music was the most important thing.

I was also involved in two music programs for kids. The first was Cazadero Music Camp, which I helped to start in 1957. Berkeley High School had the best music department of any high school I know. The kids there start playing the Brahms *First Symphony* when they are 15 or 16 years old and play it beautifully. Tom Haynes was their conductor and teacher. Bob Lutt and I, plus some other teachers from

Cazadero Music Camp 1957

Berkeley High, started the camp in Cazadero. It was a great place. I lasted 10 years, until 1965, but then it became so politicized that I had to leave. The camp was a total delight.

One of the conductor-teachers, Tom Haynes, used to pick up the kids who had been jailed for marching in parades in Berkeley, where the anti-war rallies were happening. Everywhere it was happening, but especially there. Tom and his wife finally couldn't stand it any more, so they packed up and moved to Canada. He taught sailing and played in orchestras.

The second program that I worked in was Young Audiences, Inc. We played and gave talks and demonstrations

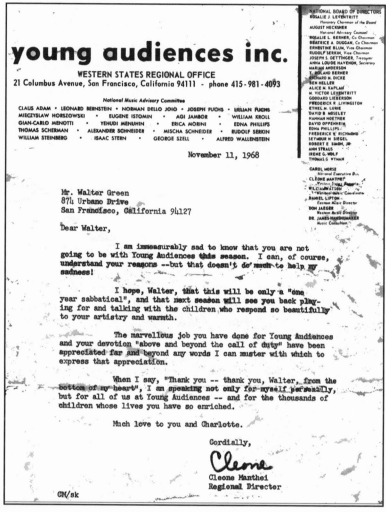

young audiences inc.

WESTERN STATES REGIONAL OFFICE
21 Columbus Avenue, San Francisco, California 94111 - phone 415-981-4093

National Music Advisory Committee

November 11, 1968

Mr. Walter Green
874 Urbano Drive
San Francisco, California 94127

Dear Walter,

I am immeasurably sad to know that you are not going to be with Young Audiences this season. I can, of course, understand your reasons --but that doesn't do much to help my sadness!

I hope, Walter, that this will be only a "one year sabbatical", and that next season will see you back playing for and talking with the children who respond so beautifully to your artistry and warmth.

The marvellous job you have done for Young Audiences and your devotion "above and beyond the call of duty" have been appreciated far and beyond any words I can muster with which to express that appreciation.

When I say, "Thank you -- thank you, Walter, from the bottom of my heart", I am speaking not only for myself personally, but for all of us at Young Audiences -- and for the thousands of children whose lives you have so enriched.

Much love to you and Charlotte.

Cordially,

Cleone

Cleone Manthei
Regional Director

CM/sk

Letter of appreciation from Young Audiences, Inc. 1968 (fire damaged)

about music to kids in the fourth, fifth, and sixth grades. That was really a musical outreach. I did that for ten years. The only reason I resigned was because with my other symphony jobs it was too much work for me.

❧

I had been promised work for the summer Pops Season and every year when Arthur Fiedler came to San Francisco

PERIPATETIC IS THE WORD for Walter Green, first bassoonist with the San Francisco Symphony orchestra, who was called to active duty with the Portland Symphony by Theodore Bloomfield when the regular bassoonist, Mrs. James Smith, became ill. . . . Ted had played with Green in Indianapolis in 1955, knew him to be one of the outstanding bassoonists in the country, made arrangements for substitution in a hurry. Upshot, Green flew to Portland for rehearsal Sunday, played in concert Monday night, left concert in time to make 12:30 a. m. plane back to San Francisco, played in concert in San Leandro Tuesday afternoon, was to fly back to Portland after San Leandro concert in time to play with symphony at concert at Willamette university auditorium Tuesday night. Let's hope he doesn't get winded!

"Just call him the flying bassoonist—Walter Green, first bassoonist with the San Francisco Symphony, has timetable, will fly, as he demonstrated by commuting between San Francisco and Portland this week in order to substitute for an ailing Portland Symphony orchestra member."—*The Oregonian*, 1958

we played for those concerts. He wasn't that good of a conductor, but in Boston he had been told that once in a great while he'd get a job conducting an orchestra for a series of concerts, so he did the Boston Pops. When he was finished with Boston, he came to San Francisco and did the same thing. Fiedler had a way of playing with an audience and they loved him, particularly when he made up as a Fire Marshall and all the rest of that theatrical stuff.

Fiedler was actually a very mean man. First of all, he needed a full water glass of scotch before he went out to conduct, and he was so stoned out of his head half the time that he didn't know what he was doing. He also had a way of being totally grouchy, especially if a woman was piano soloist. Fiedler would ride her so hard that sometime during the first rehearsal, she would get so upset by his treatment that she would burst out crying. It happened almost every time there was a woman soloist, because in those days women wanted the jobs. Fiedler wouldn't do it with someone like Gina Bachauer, because she would kill him right on the spot.

That was how Fiedler got his "jollies." I don't understand at all. I hated the Pops concerts so much that, after 22 seasons, I quit rather than play another five weeks. I didn't want to suffer through another summer and put up with the stuff that Fiedler put forth. He did, however, have a repartee that was really fabulous. I don't know what we were playing, but one night I heard the trombone player let loose with an expletive, "Maestro, why don't you go fuck yourself!" Fiedler retorted—and this is while we were playing, during a performance—"What did you say?" This trombonist again said, "Maestro, why don't you go fuck yourself?" "That's what I thought you said," replied Fiedler. When he came out with "That's what I thought you said," the orchestra cracked up. We kept playing. You better. But this kind of stuff goes on. I think that's one of the funniest things I ever experienced. The man wasn't fired after the performance, union contract or not. The punishment has to fit the crime.

In 1968 some great changes happened in orchestras all over the country. All at once, orchestra players were absolutely sick of no benefits: no retirement, no hospitalization, no overtime, no nothing. All we had was social security. When I was a member of the orchestra's Players Committee, we negotiated with the Symphony Board of Directors for some kind of remuneration for retirement. Ten of us went to see the president of the Symphony Board, who was sitting behind a big wooden desk. "Mr. President," we said, "We'd like to get compensation for retirement purposes." The President replied, "Why do you want retirement? I don't get any." That was that. That was the attitude in those days.

The unions had come to orchestras in the mid-1960s when some very intelligent people became union executives. We pushed and pushed and pushed, but management didn't want to give; they really stuck to their guns. I'm not sure, but I think it was the famous, beautiful Philadelphia

Orchestra, with that most luscious Stokowski sound, who struck first. And we, the members of the San Francisco Symphony, struck also. We were out for seven weeks and management met all our demands. At the end of the strike we got what we wanted, a 52-week season, retirement benefits, Workers' Compensation, and a base weekly salary for every member of the orchestra, including the last player in the fiddle section, just like any other working person. The triangle player might just go "bing," then goodbye, but orchestral members are not just paid for their time; they are paid for their artistry. These were benefits that workers were supposed to have, but we had never enjoyed. Now we even had paid summer vacations. There were yearly benefits for every player in the orchestra.

When the strike happened, the orchestra decided that not only weren't we going to play for peanuts any longer, but that auditions would be on the up and up, instead of arranged before anybody had a chance to play. And that sort of thing had happened often. It had happened to me during my audition for the Baltimore Symphony and it was a common occurrence for many musicians. So we now have a new auditions procedure.

When I came into the San Francisco Symphony as principal bassoonist, I auditioned against 35 of my fellow bassoonists from all over the country. Twenty-seven years later, when I retired, the person who replaced me played better than 200 other bassoonists who tried out for my job. You play in preliminary auditions and they put a screen in front of you so that no one can see who you are, if you are a man or a woman, whether you are black or Chinese or white or whatever. There are four or five different pieces of music to play. You usually start off playing the Mozart *Bassoon Concerto*. If you're really not good, the auditioning committee stops you and says, "Thank you very much. Next." The next person comes out and plays wonderfully well. So he's good

Walter Green 1969

enough to get, let's say, seven out of ten points, good enough to be in the final. That gets pared down, until there are maybe eight or ten people left. The fact that there are 200 people auditioning drives the auditioning committee totally bonkers. Management asked me to be on the audition committee for my replacement. It takes only a few minutes to recognize a great or a bad audition. Steve Dibner replaced me in the orchestra and he is a wonderful bassoonist.

Once we had auditions for the job of principal clarinetist. The man behind the screen didn't get out of the preliminaries and was voted down. He turned out to be one of the great clarinetists of the century. And we let him go. Embarrassing things happen even when you try to be super fair. He had an off day, or an off hour, or. most likely, he was nervous.

When you play regularly, the level of nervousness has something to do with the piece of music. When you're auditioning, they were all tough. There's a reason for that. Whenever somebody played an audition and was rejected, and that included me, what you felt like was that you were really not so hot. But every time that I've checked those things back and found out why a person did not get the job, the reason was always that there was somebody better. It's that simple.

Even for the best players, even if they didn't have a bad day, even if they sounded absolutely beautiful, there was someone else auditioning that day who sounded more beautiful—even though he wasn't. That's always the case, you know. And when they come up with excuses about why they didn't get the job, if you could really delve back into whether this thing is true or not, most likely the one who played the most beautifully would be the first choice of the audition committee.

After the strike, the auditioning procedure was totally changed. We had an auditioning procedure where the person auditioning played a preliminary audition for ten members of the orchestra who were chosen by the orchestra to handle the preliminary audition. These ten members were to choose those players who were voted into the final. Therefore, the only difference between the preliminary and final audition was that in the final audition the conductor had a vote and screens were removed from the stage so that the auditionee could be identified from anywhere. We found out from experience that the committee and the conductor needed to identify the auditionee in the final. Being able to see the kinesthetic motion is a great aid in passing judgment on a person's ability to play the instrument. The auditioning committee was a cross section of people who were really very honest and interested in having the orchestra be wonderful.

When I left the San Francisco Symphony, out of 250 bassoonists who auditioned only one was chosen for the job. What happened to the others? They were all saying, "Well, my reed was really soggy that day." Oh, sure.

The final auditions were also given on that day. In the old days the conductor would take the leader of a section and he and the Maestro would audition the applicant and the result was that the conductor's choice was the law. The preliminary audition was held behind a screen and you were asked to take your shoes off and audition barefoot, so no one could identify if you were a man or woman, black or white.

Once, under Krips, an audition was held for assistant principal bassoon. Well, Krips wanted to get even with me. He wanted another really great bassoonist in there. So before this auditioning procedure, he had six auditions where people were asked to play and for six times in a row he would not choose anybody. People came from all over the country to get a job like that. Management didn't pay a dime to come for the audition. You were on your own, and a plane ticket is kind of expensive. So we had the preliminary audition and only two people showed up. I jokingly asked one of my students, "Marilyn, are you going to play?" She said, "No, Walter. I've got pleurisy. I really can't." "I'm so sorry," I said, "I really wanted them to hear you."

At the end of the preliminary auditioning period, nobody would let you know what was going on. You were in the dark except for the fact that somebody was going to play for you. And you'd start out with a Mozart *Concerto*, maybe did the Beethoven *Ninth* and certainly the last movement of the Beethoven *Fourth*, which has a very difficult bassoon solo in it. I've had more nightmares playing that in concert than any other piece I know of.

Then came the final audition, which was also behind the screen. Nobody knew who the auditionee was. So they figured that if only two people were auditioning, one of them would get it, right? One person made a lot of mistakes, but had a certain amount of professionalism about him, so I wanted to hear him in the final. I wanted to go along with him and keep it as straight as possible. And the other played absolutely beautifully. No comment. I voted for the person who played beautifully to win the audition. Krips had kind of manipulated the whole thing so that only two people auditioned for this job as assistant principal.

At the end of the audition, Krips turned to the personnel manager who was there also. Krips had a big fat stogie in his mouth. "Do we have a vinner?" And Sellen said, "Yes, we do, Maestro." "Vould you give us the name of the vinner?" I thought Lenny Sharrow would to get the job. Lenny Sharrow was the principal bassoonist in the NBC Orchestra under Toscanini and he had also played under Reiner, so he had a great reputation. "Vould you tell us who the name is of who won this audition." "Yes, Miss Marilyn Mayer." My student got the job. She had told me that she had pleurisy, but then somehow she changed her mind. Turned out that she didn't have pleurisy, but tuberculosis. Which we didn't say a word about to anybody. Ray Reider, who is a doctor and has been a friend of mine ever since I came to San Francisco, took care of her during that summer. She only played for one season. They offered her a contract for second bassoon, but she decided not to accept it. She didn't want to be part of it any more.

All the orchestras across the nation changed their auditioning procedure to be like ours. Except we did give in on one thing. Something that happens, that I only partially understand myself, is that when you listen to an auditionee, you want to see them. You do not just want to hear them play. There's a kinesthetic motion and there's how they sit, how they hold the instrument, how they hold their head, their own ways of expressing themselves. All of this is part of it. You cannot give a fair audition, under any circumstance, if you do not have an auditionee in the finals in front of the screen. And after all, since the conductor is the boss, he should also be involved in choosing an auditionee, so he becomes a part of it.

There were times when the music was wonderful, yet the visual aspect was terrible. It didn't happen very often, because, when you went out in tails and a white tie and a white vest or cummerbund, you wouldn't go out there looking messy. Once or twice that I know of a person didn't change his duds and he was fired—for good reason. If you have a slob or two sitting up there, it just looks awful and it disturbs the music.

Those were the changes we made. All the schemes of management did not succeed and management never learned that if you threaten a position, everyone is psychologically and emotionally the worse for wear. These were revolutionary improvements in the orchestra.

✌

On September 15, 1969, I came home from an opera rehearsal. Charlotte and the kids were sleeping. Nancy was thirteen and I had promised that I would bring her a guitar. One of the solo singers in the opera had a guitar he wanted to sell. So he gave it to me and I wrote him a check. Just as I put the guitar down on the living room table, I heard an enormous explosion. I looked out and a car had driven into the gas main on one side of the house. I woke Charlotte and the kids up just in time and walked them over to a

David Green, Nancy Green, Walter Green, Peter Green 1970

neighbor. Then the whole house blew up and caught on fire. Everything in it was destroyed, including a bassoon, a Steinway piano, and my grandmother's things in those four boxes my mother had carried from Germany. The two priceless things I had brought from Vienna—the unique photo engraving of the Mahler *Tenth Symphony* with all of his commentaries and the congratulations from Alban Berg to Arnold Schoenberg with Schoenberg's handwriting—also burned up in the fire. I didn't have them insured. Who would have thought they would be destroyed? Their loss was intellectual, not monetary value. It happened. Everything went.

Losing some material possessions was a tragedy, but compared to what happened to Charlotte later at the end of her life, it was not such a great tragedy.

News of the fire appeared on the front page of the *San Francisco Chronicle* and the San Francisco community and all who knew and loved Charlotte rose to great heights comforting us. The house blew up on Wednesday evening and by Sunday 500 people gathered with gifts and items necessary for living.

༄

My brother Ralph was a very bright man, incredibly so. His ambition brought him to a heart attack early in his life. All his musings as a very fine psychiatrist brought him to an early grave. After finishing high school, and before going into the Army, Ralph had wanted to be a scientist. Then he was in the U.S. Army Signal Corps and went ashore at Normandy, and after that he wasn't interested in science anymore. Helping people drew his interest rather than pure science. The next few years were really tough for him and they totally affected his life. He decided that because there were so many sick people in this world, he wanted to help them with their emotional states. He decided to become a psychiatrist—"Bring war no more."

After the War, Ralph went back to school in Salt Lake as a pre-med student. But my parents were too poor to pay for his tuition, so he worked in the X-ray department while going to school at the University of Utah. The dangers from radiation were then unknown for people who worked near X-rays, and he became sterile. He graduated *cum laude* as an M.D. and took his internship at Eloise Hospital, outside of Detroit, Michigan. He married his wife, Judith, in Los Angeles. She was his second cousin. After his internship and residency, Ralph practiced psychiatry in Detroit. He and Judith lived there with Mike, their adopted son.

Ralph stayed in Detroit all his working life until he died in 1972. Then Judith had to take over the whole load. There were a lot of things to clean up at the end, because you don't expect to be gone at age 48.

Many members of the Eichengrün and Freudenstein families intermarried. The relationships in my family were: father, son, father, son, but then the father married a Freudenstein who was married to an Eichengrün who was married to a Freudenstein. But first cousins never married.

I had a cousin who lived in the country in upstate New York. When I visited her one time she said to me, "Walter, you know, Hitler did us a big favor." Aghast, I said, "What do you mean, he did us a big favor?" "If things had kept going the way they had started out," she said, "we would have all ended up as idiots." What she meant was that eventually there would have been marriages between first cousins.

Judith, her brother, Martin, and Ralph and I were practically the only ones who survived and got out of Germany alive without some kind of ailment.

Ralph was totally different from me. I go slowly, I don't rush, but he did. He was "What Makes Sammy Run." If we went downtown shopping or something, he'd always be 30 or 40 steps ahead of me. There was no way I could keep up, not in any way. He became interested in pre-Columbian art and became such a specialist that he lectured at Big Ten schools. He had a tremendous interest in and knowledge of music. He played the flute. He was, I think, the first guy in his block who had a hi-fi system. His hi-fi system took up his whole life. It was that kind of a thing.

Our relationship as brothers was not all that good. What had happened to us in Germany, where we were forced to be together all the time, without any friends, really affected the relationship. But during the last half year of his life we turned into bosom pals, and it all straightened out.

ॐ

I was chairman of the Orchestra Committee for about five years. The job of chairman was honorary. That and a quarter would not get you a cup of coffee. Not in San Francisco, nor in Vienna, either. I had a lot of work and a lot of headaches and very little prestige. Sometimes we were able to to help. There was a modern music program going on and I, as Chairman of the Orchestra Committee, was called into our manager Joe Scafiti's office the next morning. "Do you know what happened last night, Walter?" "No, Joe. What happened?" "After the last piece that we played, the very modern one, two members of the orchestra got together and played "Shave and a Haircut, Two Bits" after the end of it. I said to Joe, "Listen, I don't do your work. If you want to make an application of some kind to the union, I'll be glad to deliver it, but this is not my job. My job is to keep things going as cool as possible."

Tom Hemple and Jeffrey Kahane, the conductor of the Santa Rosa Symphony and a wonderful pianist, were the two men involved. First Jeffrey was called into Joe's office. Jeffrey apologized for his wrongdoing and gave back one week's salary. Then Hemple was called in and I was asked to go along, so nothing would happen that was beyond the pale. I told Hemple, "For God's sake, Tom. Just apologize. If you do, they'll probably give you a $100 fine or something, and that way it won't cost you your whole salary."

Mr. Gidwitz, the assistant manager of the orchestra, was there. I said to Tom, "Do you have anything to say to Mr. Gidwitz?" Tom replied, "Yes, if I had a chance, I'd do it again!" Well that meant, automatically, it had to go into arbitration. Before the arbitration, we tried again. I said, "Look, what can you give us as a deal?" Gidwitz and company said, "There are no deals. This man is fired." I said, "Wait a minute, the punishment has to fit the crime." It ended up that Hemple owed $250 to the management, but this also meant that the Symphony, as well as the Musician's Union, each had to pay the arbiters an arbitration fee of $1000. Not very smart. There were many incidents like this through the years.

⤳

In 1962, when he was 27 years old, Seiji Ozawa came to the San Francisco Symphony. It was his professional concert debut in North America. Ozawa was a guest conductor for a few years, then music director of the San Francisco Symphony from 1970 to 1976, plus another year as music adviser. He had studied under Charles Munch and Herbert von Karajan, and Leonard Bernstein had appointed him assistant conductor of the New York Philharmonic. Ozawa did everything from memory and, when it came to modern music—Stravinsky, Schoenberg—he was pretty wonderful. He jumped around the stage like an idiot, like a clown, and that has nothing to do with music, but the young Leonard Bernstein did the same thing. Ozawa was a very difficult man to get along with.

When Ozawa took over the San Francisco Symphony, he decided to rebuild. Every conductor who came in decided to rebuild. That happened seven times while I was there. Our tympanist was Roland Koloff. Seiji told him, "You know, the only thing you know how to do is dance around, when you are supposed to be playing music." Well, Roland felt the drum beat on his head and in the middle of the season, he changed from the San Francisco Symphony to the New York Philharmonic as principal tympanist, in addition to main percussion teacher at the Julliard School of Music. This is the way people change jobs in the orchestra. It's the ultimate threat, because it's not like you can walk across the street and get another job.

First of all, it is difficult to live on a musician's salary and every April 15th we received letters of re-engagement. Contracts were for one year. Ozawa lasted seven years. He was after me, too, but we worked out our disagreements. He had loads of power. When we were finally represented by a good head of the union, the conductor's power diminished some.

One of our musicians went to see Ozawa with a hidden tape recorder. Ozawa said to him, "You know why I no like you?" Herman Dortman said, "No, why don't you like me." "You remind me of my father," replied the conductor. Then Herman showed him the tape recorder. From what I understand it cost the San Francisco Symphony a large sum of money to make the settlement for Ozawa saying such a thing to an orchestra member. I have nothing but ugliness to think about that man, because ugliness was what he brought out with the orchestra.

In his last year in the orchestra, Mark Lifshey was given a bow at the end of the Beethoven *Ninth Symphony*. Then he was called into the conductor's room and told what a terrible oboist he really was. That is one way to destroy an orchestra, not to build it. If we had allowed autocratic conductors to continue this way, without protesting to management, they would have destroyed half the orchestra.

It was during this time that Ozawa threatened me. He called me in one evening after rehearsal and said, "Your family must be ashamed of how you play." He had other things to say to me, a list of things I did wrong. And he's a cold cucumber. I thought to myself, "I don't want to do this anymore." The kids were in high school, we had gone through the fire and I was tired. I decided that I wanted to play assistant principal for a few years. I still played half the concerts, and kept my overscale salary, and there was a great deal less tension in my life. So the last six years of my stint in the orchestra was as assistant principal bassoonist. I negotiated this with the union president, Jerry Spain, who was on my side, a wonderful man. My ego was not bruised by moving down one seat, because my playing was just as good as always.

I thought it would be very hard for my father. My mother had died in the meantime. You know the German mentality: if you're principal, you're great; if you're not principal, you're not so great, you're questionable. That's so much horseshit. My dad said he didn't care. Other people in the family did. My dad said, "Remember when I used to go in the servants' entrance in the insurance company? I had to live with that, Walter, and there's very little that you have to do in order to make your peace." I had already done it. His reaction was wonderful.

Ozawa could take the Berlioz *Damnation of Faust*, which I think is a wonderful piece of music, and rehearse through the whole Faust legend in seven hours and have it ready for performance. We played that every five or six years. He had a phenomenal, just incredible, memory.

Ozawa put out a recording of Beethoven's *Eroica Symphony* with the San Francisco Symphony, and the performance was really lacking. I don't mean technically, I mean musically. Ozawa was the kind of guy who would let most things go by until it came to the performance and then he wanted perfection. If things weren't right according to his standards, you would be called in at the end of the year and the maestro would read you a laundry list. The recordings he made with San Francisco and Boston are far from the greatest.

During the second world tour the Symphony and Ozawa traveled to the Soviet Union. This was a State Department tour. In Leningrad you came off the plane and a guy stood there with a rifle slung across him and a stamp to stamp your passport. He looked at you for twenty minutes, growling, then went bang, bang, bang with his stamp and you went in.

Our orchestra was kept from the Leningrad Philharmonic. The Soviet government wouldn't let their people see us and we didn't get to see them. But it was a particularly wonderful tour, in terms of whom we played with. Mstislav Rostropovich played the Dvorak *Cello Concerto* with us and at the end of the concert Ozawa pulled him out from backstage so that he could play an encore. This was the first concert that the great cellist had given in four years, because he had a gardener the Soviets didn't like. The gardener's name was Alexander Solzhenitsyn.

Rostropovich played a movement from one of the Bach *Unaccompanied Cello Suites*. I looked around and the whole orchestra was sobbing. All you could think was, "My God, where does that man get this magnificent music!" That was one of the great musical experiences of my life.

Before the concert we had sat down to dinner and eaten some of the Soviet's horrible food. After the concert, we were all invited to come to the American Embassy—the famous embassy that had so many bugs in it—and have supper. I sat next to a very stout lady who spoke very good cultured English, even if there was an accent. Her name was Prokofiev, the second Mrs. Sergei Prokofiev, who was just wonderful.

Our meals consisted mostly of cucumbers. Cucumbers for everything. Finally, on the last part of the tour, we decided we wanted to prick the old man a little bit. Ozawa wasn't that old, in fact he was very young, but he was "the old man," nevertheless. So we gathered all the cucumbers in the Aeroflot plane and put them on a big platter and presented the maestro with these jewels. He was our leader, our papa!

On our day off Mark Lifshey and I went to the Hermitage Museum to look at all the wonderful impressionist paintings. A man came running in wearing a white coat. One of the babushka ladies who took care of the Hermitage said to us, "Do you know who that is?" "No," I replied, "Who is he?" "That is Marc Chagall." He was there for the first time in 50 years. I met him in the elevator later on that evening and told him, "I want to tell you how much I love your paintings and I also played *The Firebird* in five performances with your costumes and your sets many years ago in San Diego." He said, "Thank you very much." We shook hands. I was floating on air for the next day.

We decided that the nicest thing would be to leave the Soviet Union all in one piece, which we did. You play or you're sick. Orchestras on tour are a risky proposition. Those are scheduled tours. We also went to Moscow, where all the great fiddle players, like Heifetz, came from.

We were received so wonderfully, I can't tell you, by the people in the Soviet Union. We performed a lot of Russian music and the audiences were astounded. The interpretation of the music was pretty much the same as they had heard. What was different was the technical perfection of the orchestra, which was way beyond what Europe or the Soviet Union could offer to an audience.

৵

From the Soviet Union the orchestra went to Germany and by a strange chance we gave a concert in Osnabrück. We had two free days and Charlotte and our three children were there with me because I wanted them to get an idea of what Europe was really like. We rented a car and stayed in a hotel in Lippstadt. I told my wife and children that I would show them the town, where I went to school, and the beautiful twelfth century Lutheran church. We visited the principal of my school, who told me how sorry he was about what had happened to me and to Germany. He had lost a son in France during the war, so that evil touched all of us.

As we went into the church, the organist was preparing for a wedding and said, "I would like it if you would leave now, but I can show you around tomorrow." "No, I have to get back to Osnabrück and the San Francisco Symphony. We are on a World Tour here." He said how much he loved classical music, and then he asked me my name. I said, "Walter Eichengrün." "I knew a Ralph Eichengrün," the organist said, "I went to school with him. The Ralph Eichengrün I knew wanted to become a carpenter." I told the organist that it was my brother, that Ralph had become a psychiatrist, that he had died a few months earlier. We ended up hugging each other and I released some of the hatred I felt for the Germans. But only some of it. We parted as friends, both of us very sad.

There was a plaque on the church and Charlotte stopped to read it. She asked me, "Walter, do you remember going to dinner with a Martin? I wonder if it is the same Martin who this plaque refers to." My best and only friend at the school where I had so many bad experiences was a boy named Martin. I didn't know his surname but I knew his first name was Martin. He was so very friendly and reached out to me and invited me to have dinner at his home whenever possible. We read on the placard on the church, "Here lived and preached Martin Niemöller." At the time of Hitler's greatest triumphs, Niemöller left Lippstadt to preach in a church in Berlin. Pastor Niemöller preached for a free Germany and was known for his statement, "If not now, when?" He was incarcerated in the concentration camp at Dachau. Pastor Niemöller was very much in opposition to the Nazi theories and was indeed a gentle soul who in 1945 received the Nobel Peace Prize after surviving the concentration camp. I wish I could make contact with the Niemöllers.

When one hears the words of courage spoken by a noble man, it gives you a boost, because if you look at any of the practices in the concentration camps, you think men and women are as low as they can get. Then, when you hear of someone like Martin Niemöller, who put his life on the line, you feel, well, maybe there is some hope after all:

"First they came for the Jews
and I did not speak out because I was not a Jew.
Then they came for the Communists
and I did not speak out
because I was not a Communist.
Then they came for the trade unionists
and I did not speak out
because I was not a trade unionist.
Then they came for me
and there was no one left to speak out for me."
—Pastor Martin Niemöller

Then we went to the Jewish Cemetery. I remembered the letter my mother had written to me so many years before, that a month after my encounter with the burgermeister when I was in the Army, the Jewish Cemetery in Lippstadt was put in perfect order. It wasn't. The conditions in the cemetery were just as bad as they had been the first time I was there after the war. The Germans had done nothing to alleviate the situation. We gave up on Lippstadt and couldn't get out of there fast enough. But a few years later I would make one last visit to Lippstadt.

ॐ

You build camaraderie over the years in an orchestra. There's nothing like it. The camaraderie is there between the men and the women all the way all the time. This wonderful fellowship that develops between the musicians makes the orchestra better, because playing with someone and having a very good ensemble is so important. That's a huge part of it. And you can't depend on the conductor for everything. It's not possible.

And you make such good friends, like Don Rheinberg, who played first trumpet in the San Francisco Symphony. After I would play a little solo he would lean over to me and say, "Not bad for an immigrant." One of the wonderful by-products of playing is that you end up finding someone like Bob Lehrfeld out in the sticks or somewhere and you find out that he's a great musician, that you have lots of stuff to talk over, and that you are able to exchange views with another musician.

During my last year as chairman of the Orchestra Committee, Edo DeWart became the conductor of the San Francisco Symphony. I got along fairly well with him. He knew the score, but in order to find the truth of the music he had to bury his head in the score. DeWart did okay, because he was competent, but he was also boring. I had only one encounter with him and this resulted in something quite honorable. A very nice man named Irving Mountner had incurable cancer, but he could hang on for a while and make like he was playing. Edo DeWart called him in and said, " I don't want you here any more." The only person who heard him say that was me, but I want to get that written, because no one ever talks about this sort of thing. It's ridiculous. That's why, although it's a job, it's not like other jobs.

As chairman of the Orchestra Committee I directly intervened and made a deal with Peter Pastreich, our new business manager. I said, "Look, we'll get Irving to play half the season. But you have to pay him full salary until the day he dies." Pastreich agreed to it. I said, "How can someone like DeWart make such a statement to someone who is dying of leukemia?" So I could do some good, and did, be-

THE SAN FRANCISCO SYMPHONY ORCHESTRA
JOSEF KRIPS, *Conductor and Musical Director*

PENSION FUND CONCERT
dedicated to the memory of
JAMES DAVID ZELLERBACH
Friday • April 3 • 9:00 P.M.
OPERA HOUSE

PROGRAM

Prelude to "Lohengrin"..	*Wagner*
Overture to "The Flying Dutchman"............................	*Wagner*
Overture to "Tannhauser"..	*Wagner*
Prelude and Love Death from "Tristan and Isolde".....	*Wagner*

INTERMISSION

Symphony No. 3 in E flat major (Eroica)................................*Beethoven*

THE SAN FRANCISCO SYMPHONY
JOSEF KRIPS ❀❀❀ CONDUCTOR ❀
AND MUSICAL DIRECTOR ❀❀❀❀❀
WAR MEMORIAL OPERA HOUSE ❀

"AN EVENING WITH DANNY KAYE"

For the benefit of
The Orchestra's Pension Fund

❀

Overture to 'Die Fledermaus'' by Strauss
JOSEF KRIPS, Conducting
and

?

DANNY KAYE, Conducting
(The Management assumes no responsibility for this
portion of the program.)

❀

Sunday, December 5, 1965, 8:30 P.M.

A SAN FRANCISCO SYMPHONY ASSOCIATION PRESENTATION
PHILIP S. BOONE, *President*   JOSEPH A. SCAFIDI, *Manager*

THE SAN FRANCISCO SYMPHONY
JOSEF KRIPS ❀❀❀ CONDUCTOR ❀
AND MUSICAL DIRECTOR ❀❀❀❀❀
WAR MEMORIAL OPERA HOUSE ❀

GEORGES PRETRE, *Guest Conductor*
March 3, March 4, March 5, 1965

ISAAC STERN, *Guest Artist*
February 5, February 6, February 7, 1964

SAN FRANCISCO SYMPHONY
MAGAZINE
50¢ A PERFORMING ARTS PUBLICATION MAY 1977

See Something Worth Hearing.

San Francisco Symphony 1978/79

Edo de Waart, Conductor and Music Director

Season opens November 29, 1978 War Memorial Opera House

Tickets available at the Symphony Box Office (415) 431-5400

February 1979
SAN FRANCISCO
SYMPHONY
MAGAZINE

San Francisco Symphony 1979-80

Edo de Waart, *Music Director*

Wednesday, 20 February at 8:30   Opera House, San Francisco
Thursday, 21 February at 8:15   Zellerbach Auditorium, Berkeley
Friday, 22 February at 8:30   Opera House, San Francisco
Saturday, 23 February at 8:30   Opera House, San Francisco

KURT MASUR conducting

BEETHOVEN Piano Concerto No. 5 in E flat, Opus 73, *Emperor*
  Allegro
  Adagio un poco mosso
  Rondo: Allegro ma non troppo

CLAUDIO ARRAU

Intermission

DVOŘÁK Symphony No. 9 in E minor, Opus 95, *From the New World*
  Adagio—Allegro molto
  Largo
  Molto vivace
  Allegro con fuoco

Mostly Mozart

San Francisco Symphony January 6-17
Edo de Waart Music Director
Comes to Davies Symphony Hall!

Letter of appreciation to Walter Green from San Francisco State University
1973

cause the manager went for the idea right away. It would
calm everybody, would calm DeWart down, and, frankly,
Irv was too sick to play much more. But he received his
salary and vacation pay; that didn't stop.

It was a wonderful orchestra. And it was wonderful for
the same reasons that the Vienna Philharmonic was wonderful. And that was because the Vienna Philharmonic was
also an opera orchestra in Vienna. The San Francisco Opera
Orchestra was also the San Francisco Symphony and that

saved us a lot of grief, because we had to play with big-time conductors and we all worked together. So this was a good reason for there to be pride. Whenever a new conductor would come in, he'd always be flabbergasted the way we dove into the music and got a symphonic sound. The biggest question always was, "Are we too loud?"

Up until 1980, the San Francisco Symphony and the San Francisco Opera both performed in the War Memorial Opera House. Then Louise M. Davies Symphony Hall was built, on the site of a parking lot. When we started playing in Davies Symphony Hall, we had to choose, if we weren't picked, whether we wanted to play in the Symphony or the Opera. We could not play in both anymore. That meant all the contracts had to be changed and some musicians were encouraged to go elsewhere if the conductor wasn't too happy with their playing. You couldn't belong to both because it was too much work. If you have a four and a half hour opera and dress rehearsals and then play symphony concerts, too, then God help you!

I picked the Symphony, partially because I had stood up for one of my colleagues during a negotiation thing when they were going to fire him from the Opera. I played the hero and spoke well of this man who played principal flute in the Opera. Adler never talked to me again, which is the way things go. I wouldn't kow-tow before the great Maestro.

Peter Pastreich was a very intelligent and sensitive human being. He came in as the manager of the Symphony shortly before Edo DeWart became the conductor. Skidmore, Owings & Merrill were the architects for Davies Hall. It took quite a while for them to build the hall, with the workmen going on these steel beams that were partially curved in order to get the design of this "orchestral hall." The hall rose before us and we were just blown away by the exterior design. It was absolutely wonderful.

Pastreich called me in because I was chairman of the Orchestra Committee. He said, "How'd you like to go down to Skidmore, Owings & Merrill and help them redesign the musicians' room. "Gee, that's strange," I thought. Well, it turned out that they had really mangled the backstage and didn't do a good job at all. Almost half of the orchestra personnel were women, yet they had a measly little john down there—just ugly, the sexism. I appointed a couple of people from the committee to go with me. I didn't want to do that by myself. Skidmore, Owings & Merrill were very nice to us and we went there several times and they redesigned the back of the hall, where the musicians hang out.

For the first rehearsal we were playing the Brahms *First Symphony*. When the downbeat came we couldn't hear each other. Miserable, just terrible, acoustics. They had these curtains on the side. The acoustics were designed by an architect from Denver. They found another architect to put his 10¢ worth in and that's all it was worth. More experts came and listened; there was nothing they could do immediately. And so there was nothing we could do; we had to play like that and to adjust our ears. See, the bottom of the stage, the stage floor, was wood, but under that was a layer of concrete, which doesn't resonate very much. How they could have let that pass, I'll never know. They didn't change that until the seventh or eighth year after it was built. They had spent $35 million on the building and another $8 million correcting this monstrosity. The weird thing is that the same thing happened in Denver.

The acoustics were absolutely miserable, both from a player's point of view and from the point of view of the listening audience. The problems were eventually, but not completely, corrected with big plastic panels and baffles. The last time I went there it was okay for a listener, but still not great.

But the inauguration of Davies Hall was marvelous. We had the head honcho among the workmen on these steel beams sing the *Star Spangled Banner* with us, as a soloist. His cohorts were so proud of him and of each other and of themselves, because of what they had accomplished. They did a stunning job. I don't know how the hell one can climb up there on those beams and stay up there, hour after hour. The workmen who worked on the hall were all Native Americans, most of them from the Mohawk tribe in New York. So when the man got up and sang the *Star Spangled Banner*, we were all quite moved.

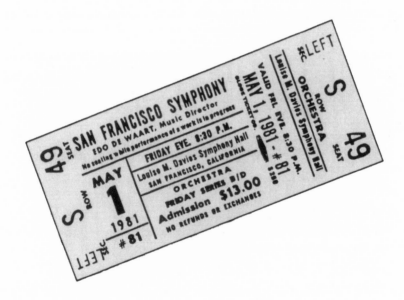

Chapter 7
Religion

Charlotte received a little inheritance in 1976 and she wanted to do two things with it. First on her list, primarily for me, was to buy us two El Al tickets to fly to Israel. That trip was one of the most important experiences in my life. But in order to explain why, I have to go way back to what is, for a religious Jewish boy, the end of childhood.

Not long after we arrived in the States, we lived in Mount Vernon, New York and it was time for my bar mitzvah. In 1939, I became a man and a blessed member of the Jewish community. I was not so much interested in the theology of what I was learning as much as having a wonderful experience with the cantor of the shul. Cantor Weinberger was one of those influences on me of music and Judaism. He trained me to perform the whole bar mitzvah service. By chance, seven years later I saw Mr. Weinberger again on the steps of the Eastman School of Music, where he was taking some rabbinic music instruction. He was so proud that I was attending the Eastman school that he totally flipped out when he saw me.

But for my mother the memory of my bar mitzvah had long-term effects. The ladies of the temple sisterhood took me to New Rochelle and bought me a suit and a tie and a white shirt for the bar mitzvah. We didn't have the money to buy new clothes for me. There was a drug store right next to where we lived. They brought me back to our apartment and said, "Oh, we forgot to get you ice cream. Let's take you downstairs for some." Mom started crying as soon as they left. It's hard to give. It's hard to receive. That's a good part of it. My parents had been good middle-class Jews in Germany, and now they had no choice but to accept charity. My mother was ashamed and her pride was shattered. No matter what the women from the sisterhood did, no matter their good, and honorable, intentions, this happened. It's very hard to stay even when you come into a new country and have to deal with something like this.

Then, after we moved to Salt Lake City, something really ugly seemed to happen in our lives. There was this terrible "misunderstanding" between the eastern European Jews and the German Jews. For whatever the reasons, whether it was because they got there last or because there were prejudices held over from the "old countries," or because an odd and unique situation existed in Salt Lake City, German Jews were looked down upon by other non-German Jews. It was a situation that I didn't understand then and don't understand now, but I know my family, and other German Jews, encountered animosity from non-German Jews in Salt Lake City. I can't believe this was a universal attitude across the United States at the time, but I know it existed during the years I lived in Utah. Maybe if you didn't experience it, you can't understand it.

Jewish life in Salt Lake City was thriving. How many Jews could there have been in Salt Lake City? A lot more than one could imagine. There were actually three congregations that were functioning well: Orthodox, Conservative, and Reformed. We were part of the Reformed for a while. We were treated as Jews who had brought a lot of pain onto themselves by being very snobbish during the years when Jews had left Russia and Poland and Czechoslovakia, and God knows where. And they were right. The German Jews living in Germany were too interested in "*Kultur*" and were mean to the Polish and Russians as they came through there to get to the United States.

The Jewish communities in Salt Lake City were very helpful to us but, like all German Jews who moved there, and there were quite a few families, our status was low. The Polish or Russian or Rumanian or Hungarian Jews who had arrived earlier regarded German Jews as inferior. Oh, they were certainly charitable. The Jewish Agency, which welcomed us to Salt Lake and found us a furnished apartment, was wonderful. But if we couldn't afford tickets, we had to sit in the back of the bus—in the back of the temple—on the High Holidays.

My dad always had a job, but he only made $50 a week. For 20 years he asked for raises but didn't get them, and he had to listen to his non-German Jewish boss make remarks about the German Jews "who thought that they were everything."

We got along well with the Mormons, who were out to help anyone who came into their church. Jews were one of the lost tribes of Israel and the Mormon Temple, as well as their occupants, were there to help us. And although we didn't fit into the community life until much later, there were enough refugees trying to become Americans that no one ever felt lonely for the good old days and the good old country. On the contrary, we felt wonderful to have escaped from the horror in Europe. The German Jewish community members were helpful to each other in getting settled in a new land.

I was very upset about the way we were treated. I just wanted my search not to be dependent on people feeling sorry because I had to undergo such a thing twice: once from the German Nazis and the second time from my own brethren of the Jewish congregation in Salt Lake City. So I didn't want to be a Jew any more. The heck with that. I decided being Jewish was for the birds and through the next few years I tasted everything various religions had to offer. I became Presbyterian, Episcopalian, Buddhist, and with my mother's help, landed as a Unitarian.

My father remained a good Jew until his death, and he was truly devoted. This devotion carried him through 20 years of very hard work. All good things about Judaism were with him. But the only time I ever went to temple was with my dad to Yom Kippur service—the Day of Atonement—and I did it just for him. My mom wouldn't go. She was an unofficial Unitarian.

I started looking. Where would I feel comfortable? The Mormon Religion wasn't the way, not for me. Episcopalian was not right, either. I couldn't envision myself belonging to one of these churches where they'd say, "Walter Green, he's the, you know, the Jew." I just didn't want that, so I kept switching from one religious belief to the next.

I went to the Methodist Church and I finally married a Methodist, Charlotte, who was already a Unitarian. At the end of our marriage ceremony Charlotte's aunt said to her, "Charlotte, why did you stray? You didn't mention the name of God, even once." She really strayed by marrying me. Boy, did she ever! Little did she know I was going to surprise her later.

I was very impressed by Catholicism and its ritual. Then I went to the Episcopal Church, which didn't have half of the stuff in it that Catholicism had, but was somewhat related. One of my dear friends in the Army, Louis Hasbrook, was an Episcopalian. He lived in Ogdensburg, a small town in upstate New York. He helped me financially all the way through Eastman. I had met Louis in the counter-intelligence corps. He was older than me and he returned to the States much earlier than I did. But while he was in Vienna, with my small amount of musical knowledge, I walked him through the Vienna State Opera and through the symphonies of Beethoven and he was forever grateful for this. Because there was only one Protestant church in Vienna, he went there. He asked me to come along and I did. I don't remember what kind of church it was, probably Lutheran.

Louis and I remain friends to this day. He came from a wealthy home. His parents were both dead and he was brought up by a tutor and went to boys' schools. His family wasn't just New York aristocracy. It goes further, to Roosevelt and all those people who fit in. I remember going to a party in Albany and meeting a past governor of New York State. It was that level of society. At any rate, that brought together my love of pageantry and ritual and I felt fairly comfortable with the Episcopal Church.

But then I found out about Unitarianism—from my mother, although she was not able to let go of her Jewish faith. It was too difficult for her. She couldn't do that. When I was home for Christmas she begged me to put a Christmas tree in our house. Which I did, with great glee at my dad's expense. So I slowly started to turn to a wonderful, liberal religion, concerned with many social issues, as well as a lot of beauty in whatever they prayed to, because Unitarians pray "To whom it may concern." Which is marvelous!

When I was in the Unitarian Congregation in San Francisco, I loved everything, especially the minister, Harry Scofield, who was a unique human being and a very warmhearted soul. When he retired, I left, because there really wasn't a minister that I felt comfortable with. But I remained a Unitarian for many years, although on occasion some event would occur to question my complacency.

One night at the opera we were playing Puccini's *Tosca* and our principal bass player, Phil Karp, said, "Walter, would you like to meet Jan Peerce?" who was singing Cavaradossi that evening. I said, "Of course I would." He said, "Follow me at intermission." We went up the stairs to Peerce's dressing room and knocked on the door "Come in," he said, "come on in! Have a few apples with honey. I just got through at the Synagogue, singing and praying all day, and now for the New Year, to keep my throat in good shape, I'm going to have to eat more apples and more honey." So I stood there. I was tongue-tied. I have never been closer to my dreams in my life.

We talked and he chatted, about New York, about his cousin, Richard Tucker, another famous tenor. They were both marvelous. I remembered the criticism of Tucker's voice, because Europeans didn't think he could enunciate correctly, even though he had a voice that was—glory! We kept talking and Peerce was so nice and said, "Come and see me again, boys. I'll tell you, because you made such a good visit here, I am going to sing a special thing in the second act of Tosca." Walking out of the dressing room, Phil and I looked at each other and said, "What is he doing? This is a performance." Well, the opera's hero, Cavaradossi, Peerce's role, gets tortured in the middle of the second act and he lets out these terrible groans. What Phil and I heard, sitting back in the pit, was "*Oy.*"

Another time when Peerce was in San Francisco it was time for what is called *yartzeit*, the yearly celebration of the death of a relative, usually a parent. You need ten Jewish men for a *minyan*, a gathering. Jacob Krakmalnik was concertmaster of the Opera as well as the Symphony. He was a very famous concertmaster, not only in San Francisco, but in other orchestras as well. Jake came around and said, "Walter, come into Mr. Peerce's dressing room. He wants to say *yartzeit* for his mother." So thirteen or fourteen of us crowded in there and Peerce said, "Thank you so much for coming, boys. I'm going to say *yartzeit* now." He prayed, and then started to sing. Our business manager, Joe Scafidi, knocked at the door. I was at the door and said, "You can't come in here." Bang! I shut the door in his face. Joe yelled, "What's going on in there, Walter?" "None of your business." Bang! It happened about five or six times. The only time I was able to talk back to Joe Scafidi was when Jan Peerce had his *yartzeit*. It was a wonderful moment, talking back to Joe, but Peerce's religious devotion shook me.

In 1976 Charlotte and I used those two tickets purchased with her inheritance and flew to Israel, El Al from New York. In the morning, as we approached Europe, I began to feel very strange, thinking about the place to which many of my Jewish family had been able to escape. Several passengers jumped around the airplane to find the sunrise so they could say the morning prayers. As we flew over the Mediterranean Sea, they moved to the other side of the plane to watch for the tip of Israel from the sky. Just before we got to Israel, one of the *copadniks* offered me a sandwich, because he felt that the sandwich made by my dear wife was not kosher enough.

As we flew over the land of Israel, before our descent to the airport in Tel Aviv, I started to cry. I began sobbing and couldn't stop. Charlotte asked me what was wrong. I said, "Do you realize what's happening to me at this moment?" "Well," she said, "What is it?" "I'm flying over the land that was promised to the Jewish People, to me," I said, "And it isn't ours yet, nor ever will be . . ." I'll tell you one thing, I don't care how much you believe or don't believe, for a Jew to fly over Israel puts one's beliefs to the test.

If that wasn't enough of a huge introduction to Israel, there was more to come. I walked out of the airport and felt the warm sun beating down on me. A man was standing on the sidewalk. He looked at me and slowly and softly said, "Walter?" And I said, "Yossi." This was the first time I had seen my cousin since 1938. Then we fell into each other's arms. It was one of the most tender moments in my life, seeing the physical certainty that we had survived, all of us. Can you imagine the emotion? It would make a believer of anybody.

In the car was Yossi's brother, Abraham, who had driven for three hours from his kibbutz to greet me. Josef Zur lived in a kibbutz most of his life in Israel and is still in a kibbutz located in Negev Desert. We went there to visit my father's sister, Marta, Yossi's mother. All of this had a strong religious significance for me. I mean, these were my people!

—from Schumann *Symphony No. 1*

Chapter 8
To the Mendocino Coast

The second item on Charlotte's list was to buy a retirement home for us. We had spent a couple of vacations in Mendocino County, mostly in Gualala, and we loved it. We had thought about the mountains, or the valley, thought about all kinds of places, but we liked the Mendocino Coast the best. I saw an advertisement in the *San Francisco Chronicle* about a "lovely home" for sale in Manchester, north of Point Arena. I said to Charlotte, "Do you want to live somewhere by the ocean?" Charlotte said she would be delighted to go to look at it. That weekend we decided to take a drive. My cousin's son, Amikan, was visiting us with his girlfriend and they were happy to get out into the country. They were living in Pasadena, where he was studying for a post-doctorate at Cal Tech.

The advertisement for the house came from a real estate office in Elk, just north of Manchester. We drove north on Highway One, to Mid-Coast Realty, owned by Polly Scanlon. Charlotte and I waltzed into the office and Polly's assistant, Phyllis Grissim, an absolutely wonderful lady, offered to show us the house in Manchester that was listed in the *Chronicle*. We looked at the house, and made an immediate offer to buy it, which Phyllis took on the spot. Shortly after we made the offer, her husband had a heart attack and she had to leave Elk to take care of him in his last hours. Polly took over the escrow and I was delighted by her, in terms of how she took care of us and our real estate needs.

The three of us got on so well together that Charlotte said to me, "I don't feel like going down to the concert in the City. Why don't you get a ticket for Polly and take her to the symphony. You can play the concert and go out for a drink afterwards." I agreed to do it. So I went out with Polly and we had a wonderful time. Her daughter, Sioban, who accompanied us, didn't want us to have a drink. So instead we all had ice cream, which was much better anyway. I became more acquainted with Polly through the real estate transaction for the Manchester house. After the escrow closed, Charlotte and I invited Polly and Phyllie over to the house for dinner and it was a joyous celebration.

That house was not meant to be just a retirement house; it was a small place for Charlotte and me to relax and enjoy the country air. When Charlotte looked out the front window she saw a meadow, and beyond the meadow there was a barn, and that intrigued her. She said, "That's just like an Indiana barn, in Crown Point," where she was born.

〜〜

Charlotte had always been a very healthy person. One morning in 1981 she had a terrible headache and lay down on the couch. When I came home after the rehearsal, in the afternoon, she was still lying in the same position on the couch. I asked her if she'd had any lunch and she said, "No." I said, "Would you like some scrambled eggs?" She said, "Yes, I'll have the scrambled eggs." I went into the kitchen, made the eggs, then took them to her. "Here you are, Honey," She ate one bite and that was all. She wouldn't eat any more.

I finally called an ambulance, because I didn't think she was breathing. When the ambulance came, Phyllis Gomez, our neighbor and a good friend, came round to see whether she could help. The ambulance took Charlotte to Kaiser Hospital on Geary Street and the doctors tried resuscitating her, to make her breathe again. They told me she needed to

165

go to a different hospital, one that had more equipment to help her through. So she was taken to Kaiser Hospital in Redwood City, where she could get a CAT scan.

I was told that she had a huge growth on her brain. They kept her on a respirator. For four days our kids and I sat in Charlotte's room, singing Israeli songs to her, which she loved. She was in a coma the whole time. Then the neurosurgeon said, "Mr. Green, your wife is just on the edge of not breathing at all." So that was it. Nancy, David, and Peter sat there, as their mother died. We felt very, very sad.

Charlotte had been a social worker at the University of California Medical Center up on Parnassus Street. When Nancy, Peter, and David were at least in junior highschool, Charlotte went back to work at the Neonatal Center. She was second only to the famous psychiatrist and social worker, Elisabeth Kübler-Ross, who specialized in death and grieving. Charlotte did revolutionary work and became quite famous in San Francisco. She insisted that a room should be there for parents and children who were hurting and grieving. She wanted to make sure the parents had a chance to love and caress their premature babies and children. She taught the doctors at the hospital how to grieve. Charlotte was a warmhearted person who would work four days a week, then on the fifth day she would lie in her bed and cry over all the things that she was part of with these little tiny tikes and their survival or nonsurvival.

More than 500 people, including many nurses and doctors, attended the memorial service. I was comforted by my children and also by Charlotte's brother and sisters, who took part in the service. I received condolence letters, including a marvelous letter from Senator Diane Feinstein, from all kinds of people who had worked with Charlotte and who knew her as the giving person she was. The flags in San Francisco flew at half-staff because of the work she had done during her twelve-year tenure at the University. There is a room on the 15th floor of the hospital, the Charlotte Green Room, that was dedicated to her about a year after her death, with a plaque in her honor.

We buried Charlotte's ashes in Ocean Beach. Anybody can make anything of that that they want to, but that's what we did. We felt we wanted to do that and no more.

Charlotte and I lived together for 27 years and at the end of the 27th year, she decided to go her own way. I mean that figuratively. We always said that her missions on this earth were fulfilled, that she had to go somewhere else to go on beyond that and that's why she died so young. My kids were just entering adulthood when Charlotte died and it was a difficult time for all of us.

The minister of our church was Harry Sholefield. He was into all kinds of social issues. Just before the memorial service began, he pulled me aside and said, "Walter, I'll bet you'll be married within a year and a half." I said, "Harry, you are out of your mind. How can you say that?" "It's been my experience," he said, "that when someone who's 50 or 55 loses a mate, that someone else will come along. They have nothing to prove. Consequently, they can fall in love with someone else and get married." Which is exactly what happened to me. And not only to me, but later on it happened to Harry Sholefield, too. Which was quite amazing.

Charlotte brought so many blessings in every way to my life. She had the ability to bring people together to share their happiness or their grief. She was a marvelous mother. A very liberal person who was just my ideal of a wife.

◌

My kids and I took over the house in Manchester. We slept on the floor at night. We had absolutely no furniture, and only a few cups and saucers and stuff. Peter was 18, David was 20, and blessed Nancy was 22. My accountant had talked badly about Point Arena and all the hippies, so I got rid of him. That made me feel good.

A few months later Polly Scanlon wrote me a little note. She had never intruded on my privacy, but she asked if I would like to take a walk in the woods. I said I would. But, knowing that I was still in a state of deep grief, she said "There's just one condition, that you don't talk on the walk. Whatever happens in your head, that's fine. But just walk." It was delightful. We went into the Pygmy Forest and down this steep grade and took the path at Van Damme State Park. We did talk a little, but mostly just walked in silence. We saw a bunch of three-leafed clover, Redwood Sorrel, shaped like hearts all along the trail, and it was pure magic. Polly was just incredibly caring and truly offered her deepest sympathy.

I saw Polly quite often after that. Her knowledge about death and dying was enormous, because she had lost two daughters to leukemia—one at age five and one at age ten. She was truly, profoundly intelligent about death and dying and losing someone.

In the meantime, I was going into therapy in San Francisco and had a therapist who was studying Chinese because she was going to go to China to do therapy there. I spent eight months with her, talking about grief and grieving, trying to accept my incredible loss.

A lot of people tell me that they consider me very lucky because I've had two marriages that were so wonderful. Yes, I'm incredibly fortunate and lucky to be full of joy after such tragedy. That kind of luck rarely strikes once, let alone twice.

Polly and I were married in 1982. The wedding was at Harry Sholefield's house in Lucas Valley. That wonderful Unitarian minister had been so prophetic when he had said to me, "You'll be married in a year." But as I drove to Lucas Valley, I suffered much of the way from terrific angina. That was the second time I felt those pains since I left the orchestra. The first time was in 1975 when I carried the bassoon from the car to Davies Symphony Hall. Apparently

Walter and Polly Green, on their wedding day 1982

Polly didn't notice anything unusual, and the ceremony was something astounding, at least to us. The wedding party consisted of Polly and me and our children and Polly's mother. That was it. Harry was a very artistic human being—a real *mensch*.

Polly and I had an incredible honeymoon, which started out in Israel. At an Eichengrün celebration in Haifa I met cousins who used to push me in my baby carriage almost 60 years ago. Then Polly and I went on to Egypt, and down the Nile River to Luxor. It was the most amazing trip. I know that I walked up 186 steps in the Great Pyramid and was really not out of breath. There were no heart problems during the honeymoon. It was the greatest traveling I ever did, from beginning to end. I have a picture of Polly in the Golan Heights, right by the UN and stuff like that. She had done a lot of traveling, had trekked in Nepal in the 1970s. A wonderful travel companion.

After we returned I started getting angina again and began going to the doctor. The doctors at Kaiser told me that my aortic valve had stenosis and was not working well. "One of these days," the doctor said, "we're going to have to replace this. Not yet, but one of these days." I said, "Okay. Yeah. Maybe. Maybe not." He gave me propranolol, which was a real heart saver. If you took propranolol or its common name, Inderal, you probably didn't need anything else to counter the angina. For all these years I've taken Inderal, with no side effects.

But the thing is, I'm very susceptible to the drug. I had a concert to play one Sunday. I took the Inderal the night before, for the first time. It made me feel like I was dead. My arms were cold. My heart was going about 40 or 50 beats a minute. It slows the heartbeat down and opens it up. I went and played the recital. The bassoon was here and the bassoon was there, sometimes, and there was an audience out there, somewhere. Nobody noticed. I was able to play the bassoon, even though the rest of me wasn't there.

I was supposed to play a recital in Carnegie Recital Hall. I had set that as my goal, after I had left the Symphony. I was going to play the Mozart *Two Bassoon Sonata*, which is a fairly early work, K.192; the Hindemith *Bassoon Sonata*; and the Saint-Saens *Sonata for Bassoon and Piano*. It was a fine program. While practicing for the recital in Marin I experienced severe angina and drove to Kaiser Hospital in Marin. The next morning the cardiologist, Dr. James Slaughter, came into my room and said, "Mr. Green, about your recital . . ." I said, "Yes, what about it?" "Well, we just looked at all the findings from your tests and you're not going. You're not leaving the hospital."

We drove down to Kaiser in San Francisco. They did an angiogram and found that the aortic valve was almost totally shut. Well, Dr. Terrence McEnany did the surgery, which went well, except one of the sutures in the heart gave way and they had a code blue and had to do the surgery over again. I was on the table for seven hours. The doctor asked me what kind of a valve I would like. I could have a mechanical valve, which would never be changed, but I would have to take a drug with it that isn't too good for you. I asked, "What would you do, Doctor?" He said, "I would only go with a pig valve, because with the mechanical valve, you are liable to have troubles with your heart, and with all kinds of diseases. The mechanical valve isn't perfected yet, especially for people over 50," which included me. I asked the doctor how long the pig valve would last. He said from five to seven years. I said, "Well, I'll take the pig valve. I don't want a stroke," which might happen with the mechanical valve.

So I never gave a solo recital in Carnegie Hall, but if it weren't for the outstanding care I received, I wouldn't be here today. The medical staff treated me with great dignigy. Twenty years now, and it's still going strong, really well. I get checked every year. Everything is good to this day. I recently went in to see Dr. Jason Kirkman, who pronounced me well. Not only is he a good doctor but also a hell of a good pianist. I feel happy under his care.

—from Hummel *Concerto in F major for Bassoon and Piano*

KAISER FOUNDATION HEALTH PLAN, INC., NORTHERN CALIFORNIA REGION

PLANNING FOR HEALTH

WINTER 1990-91

INSIDE: CONTROLLING HEALTH COSTS, 'TIRED BLOOD,' CARDIOVASCULAR SURGERY

SAN RAFAEL/PETALUMA/NOVATO

Heart surgery permits symphony bassoonist to bike again (see page 9).

Photograph of Walter Green
on the cover of the Kaiser Foundation Health Plan Magazine,
which featured Walter's retirement from the San Francisco Symphony
and his retirement life after heart surgery.

Chapter 9
Marin
1983 — 1984

I had played in the San Francisco Symphony for twenty-seven years and twenty-four years in the San Francisco Opera. It was time to quit. It was a good thing that my dear wife, Polly, had enough in her pay check to help us through, because I could never have made it on my own when I decided to retire at age 57. I couldn't get Social Security until I was 62. When I finally made up my mind I was going to leave, I went into Peter Pastreich's office. He had coffee and cake ready for us. We chatted and I said, "You know, Peter, I want to quit." "Well," Pastreich replied, "Usually when somebody wants to quit the orchestra, the conductor and management want them to quit, too, so we give them recompense for those years. We pay them to leave. But we can't do that with you, Walter. We owe you too much. We want you to stay. You made the backbone of the orchestra." He gave me a pension benefit for five years until my regular pension kicked in.

It was really time to quit because I did not want to get sour about music and, once in a while, I'd find myself getting that way and I didn't like it. It's the great muse and the muse should not be desecrated and that's as eloquent as I can say that. Twenty-seven years in the San Francisco Symphony was enough to make me want to do something beyond that. Beyond is not meant as a criticism. Beyond is that there must be something else, something different.

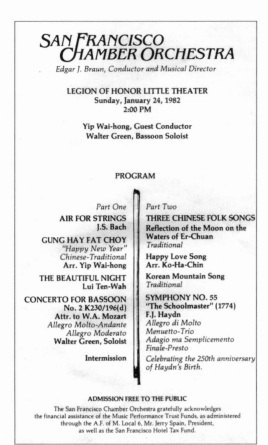

I planned to retire at the end of the 1983 season. I had no idea what I was going to do, but I knew I would do something.

What happened was that on the very day I made the decision to quit the San Francisco Symphony, I received an offer from the Marin Symphony to play principal bassoon, which I did for the next sixteen years. The Marin Symphony is a community orchestra, but it has a lot of professionals in it, and the conductors were excellent. I really enjoyed myself, without a lot of heavy pressure.

So for one year I did both the San Francisco Symphony and the Marin Symphony, which occupied many hours of work. The conductor of the Marin Symphony, Sandor Salgo, liked my playing and he liked me, personally. He was a nice gentle old man who must have thought, "Here's nice gentle old Walter Green who will play bassoon for me." Salgo called me and said, "I want you." And I said, "Thank you, I'll take the job."

During the first day in Marin I got a reminder that I had made a wise choice. Charles Meecham, the Marin Sym-

phony concert-
master, came up
to me and said,
"W a l t e r , y o u
know that I left
the San Francisco
Symphony while
you were there." I
said, "Yes, I was so
surprised that
you left then."
"Well," he said,
"you're to blame
for it." I said,
"What are you
talking about?"
He said, "Do you
remember that
time when Krips
jumped off the
podium and spit
in your face?" I
said, "I sure do!"
Meecham said, "I

Recital

Bassoon and Piano

Walter Green-Bassoon   Roxanne Michaelian-Piano

Sonata III C Major   Bassoon and Piano
Antonio Vivaldi 1648-1741

Largo
Allegro
Largo
Allegro

Sonata   Bassoon and Piano
Paul Hindemith 1918-1962

Lightly Moving
Slow
March
Pastorale

Ballade G Minor   Opus 23   Piano
Fredric Chopin 1810-1849

Intermission

Two Habraic Studies   Bassoon
Marvin Feinsmith 1926-

Concerto II   Bb Major   Bassoon and Piano
Wolfgand Amadeus Mozart 1756-1791

Allegro
Romance
Rondo

A Recital for Bassoon and Piano,
Elk Methodist Church, May 9th, 1982

live in Marin County and after the rehearsal I was driving
up the Waldo Grade, coming out of San Francisco. I stopped
the car in the middle of the Waldo Grade, got out and threw
up, got back in the car and drove all the way home, thinking, 'I don't need this. I don't need anyone to treat me like
that. I quit.'" The next day he quit.

The benefit for me was that I could ease off more slowly
after quitting the San Francisco Symphony, rather than just
dive right out. I knew it could be very dangerous just to
retire; it's not unusual for people to retire and die and that
worried me. I remembered the case of Sherman Walt, prin-

THE MARIN SYMPHONY

SANDOR SALGO, CONDUCTOR

Flourishing

84/85 SEASON

SUNDAY SERIES & TUESDAY ENCORE SERIES
7:30 P.M., MARIN CENTER AUDITORIUM

cipal bassoonist of the Boston Symphony, who died eight months after he retired. Walt was in the backyard when his wife drove the car out of the garage and drove right over him. There was a second bassoonist of the San Francisco Symphony, who bid me such a valiant farewell by saying "No one will ever remember you now." He died eight months after he left the orchestra. And a wonderful freelance bassoonist in New York, Eli Carmen, came down with a cold and pneumonia and died eight months after he stopped playing. That's how strenuous playing in an orchestra full-time really is and what can be its aftermath if you just stop.

When I retired, I wanted something in place that I could go to, and that was the Marin Symphony. It was perfect. Just six, eight concerts a year and lots of rehearsals, even though there was a long drive from Elk, where Polly and I were living, to get to rehearsals. I joined the Marin Symphony in 1982. At the first performance that I played, Polly was sitting in the audience and overheard a gentleman in front of her say, "I hear we have a world-class bassoonist coming into the orchestra." Needless to say she was impressed.

The Marin Symphony plays in the hall behind the Frank Lloyd Wright building at the Marin County Civic Center in San Rafael. It's a nice place to play, but it doesn't have the greatest acoustics. You can tell it's Frank Lloyd Wright by the looks, but acoustics was not one of his stronger points.

Sandor Salgo knew of my playing because I had played casual jobs with him in the past. Casual jobs are when somebody offers you a job to play a Beethoven symphony or some other piece of music and the contrac-

Walter Green 1987

tor wants you to play principal bassoon. It's almost like playing a symphony concert somewhere. An example was the Pops season with Arthur Fielder in the Civic Auditorium in San Francisco. You go into the auditorium and the contractor, the personnel manager, goes clap, clap, clap and you take your seat and the music is there in front of you and you begin playing when the conductor gives the downbeat and hopefully you finish after a three-hour session.

Once there were a series of concerts called the San Francisco Symphony Plays Jazz. We played with Ella Fitzgerald and with Peggy Lee and Oscar Peterson and others. These people were soloists with us and they probably made lots of money. We were paid at union scale. We played with whoever was put in front of us. I played with Salgo in Palo Alto when we did a whole session for two or three weeks

Walter Green 1988

with the Stuttgart Orchestra. We did, among other things, Mozart's *Abduction from the Seraglio*. Wonderful opera.

I mentioned Eli Carmen, who played principal bassoon for a few years with the NBC Orchestra, but mostly he just played casual jobs. The most the average casual musician, who was a sideman, made in San Francisco was $20,000 a year. That ain't much! So then they go down to Modesto and play with the Modesto Symphony—same people—and they'll make another something. It adds up to about

$20,000, at the highest. So it's not very lucrative, but you have some damn good players. There is a group of about 30 or 40 men and women who play these concerts in Northern California and they are all playing casual jobs. Another orchestra that uses casual players is the Santa Rosa Symphony. Two of my students play first and second bassoon with the Santa Rosa Symphony. Jeffrey Kahane is the conductor there now, and Jeff is very good. Everyone in the orchestra loves him and he's going to be great.

That's how casual musicians get by, but they can't make enough money. That's their complete earnings except for teaching, and in teaching you don't make much money. It just doesn't happen. When I first came into the San Francisco Symphony and Opera, the principal cellist was Boris Blinder. He came from the old country, and had a thick Russian accent. He took hold of me and hugged me and kissed me and said how glad he was that I was with them. I asked Boris if it was possible to teach in San Francisco. He said, "Yes, darlink, certainly!" "Do you teach?" He said, "Yes, I do." I said, "How much money do you make?" He answered, "$50 a student." Now, you know what $50 was in 1950. I queried, "How many students do you have?" "None!" he said. I thought that was just a great retort.

I taught at the San Francisco Conservatory and at San Francisco State University. That's a side job totally, just like when I taught at the University of Utah in Salt Lake and Butler University in Indianapolis. Extra money in my pocket. I taught bassoon, of course, but I also had a minor in Woodwind Pedagogy so I could give lessons in the other woodwinds. The Symphony rehearsals went from 10:00 a.m to 1:00 p.m. I would come home from rehearsal about 1:30. After I got a bite to eat and took a half-hour nap, I would teach for a couple, three hours. That went on four days a week. Then I would play the evening performance. This is how we piled up 70 to 80 hours of work a week. I used to have, on the average, eight students a week. That was just San Francisco State, which used to have the best music department. They wanted me to continue teaching, but I didn't want to leave Elk; it was my choice. My replacement bassoonist in the San Francisco Symphony took over most of my students.

At that time Proposition 13 was going hot and heavy. Music in the schools was at a low ebb. That's when it all started—the struggle for music in the schools. I went to the Board of Education and gave a plea talk about not taking the liberal arts out of the curriculum. It didn't do a damn bit of good. It's just the most discouraging part of music. You see youngsters who are quite talented and you get a feel for them after awhile. They start blossoming. I had one student who studied with me for four years and then went on to play principal bassoon for Herbert Von Karajan in a pickup youth orchestra.

When one had a fairly good student who was interested, it was an absolute pleasure to teach. Until the state got into the business of evaluating the teachers, it was great. After that, it was not so good any more. It was very much like today, when someone like a secretary from the Department of Education comes in, sits down and evaluates how you relate to the student, and has absolutely no idea how to teach music to a student.

I had a marvelous student named Joseph Handlon, who was my age, which was pretty unusual. He was a psychologist at Stanford University Medical School and taught the psychiatrists there. He had played oboe professionally in a WPA Orchestra in the Thirties. He decided he wanted to learn to play the bassoon and became my student. He absorbed things beautifully and is an eloquent guy. He and his wife moved away to Cleveland, to Case Western University. Now they live in Santa Barbara and we remain bosom pals to this day. I asked him to write the introduction to this book. I hold him in the highest esteem.

Walter Green 1990

I taught for twenty-seven years. Whenever I could get a teaching job somewhere, I grabbed it, unless it was impossible to fit into my schedule. What I really loved about teaching is the one on one—one teacher and one student. My lessons helped to direct a student into the right channels. No one could tell me how to teach or what to teach. I also liked stopping at the end of a semester and just taking a few weeks off.

⤳

The Marin Symphony was a very good orchestra. Even though many amateurs were in it, the organization was not overpowered by them. There were just some very good players and some really good professionals. Our principal clarinetist, Arthur Austin, was superb.

Occasionally guest conductors came to Marin and quite often well-known soloists. The Marin Symphony performed during the summer and once we played the Tchaikovsky Violin Concerto with Itzak Perlman. Not a bad fiddler. Naturally we had some secondary soloists who were still halfway down the line, but on their way up.

Salgo was anything but a task master. We got away with murder, meaning that we could have played better, but that happens anywhere. If I'm playing first kazoo in the New York Philharmonic, I could do better. It's always true and it was true in Marin, maybe a little bit more so.

The conductor that followed Salgo was Gary Sheldon, who was a very good musician and a very good conductor. He was a little distant from the members of the orchestra and sometimes one wished that he would not be so distant. I hope that the reader knows by now that I prefer matters of the heart.

Young musicians today are generally better than they were when I was a young man. If you listen to the Marin Symphony horn section, it is much better than the San Francisco Symphony horn section was 50 years ago. The reason is that young musicians come into the Marin Symphony and often end up with jobs in the San Francisco Symphony. The Marin Symphony is a good training ground.

Marin was a wonderful group of people and a good conductor and that makes for good music-making because everyone feels good toward everyone else—or mostly. I was often invited to Erica and Larry Posner's home for Sunday supper before the Marin Symphony concerts. Larry was a doctor and played the clarinet. Erica was a psychologist and played the cello. There was always joy and cheerful camaraderie. Larry had a particularly wild sense of humor, which came out dry. Aside from that, he was a very good internist! But imagine, someone like that who put in all those years of practice so he could play second clarinet in Marin, and maybe a casual chamber music job sometime. Those were the kind of people in that orchestra, and it was a real pleasure to make music with them. They were wonderful, all of them.

An example of the loveliness of those musicians: One Saturday Polly and I drove to Marin, the night before the rehearsal the next day. On Sunday morning Polly stayed at the hotel while I played. I opened my bassoon case and looked at my bassoon. "I can't possibly play any more," I said, "I can't play. It's not possible. I'm getting old." My heart was pounding, beating hard. As the Maestro walked by he said to me, worriedly, "How are things, Walter?" I said, "I'm sorry. I can't play any more. I feel sick." He said, "Just sit down for a minute." I sat down, then he ran to get one of the bass players, who was an internist. She was very nice to me, encouraging, and listened to my heart without a stethoscope, just to see what was cooking. Then she drove me back to the hotel and Polly and I went home.

That was the end of Marin for me. Except just recently, when I went back stage before a concert. The people flipped when they saw me, which was really gratifying. First my two students immediately came up and greeted me, "Walter, why didn't you let us know you would be here?" "Oh, Walter, how are you feeling!" And on and on.

Chapter 10
Mendocino & The Mendocino Music Festival
1983 — 2004

Not long after Polly and I were married, we decided it was time for us to buy a house for ourselves, one that didn't have a background or a history of Charlotte. No ghosts. We saw this charming farmhouse on the side of a hill, five miles south of Elk, that overlooked the whole Pacific Ocean, and we bought the place. We rented out the Manchester house, then sold it last year. We stayed in the "new" house 14 years. The joy of that incredible view! I don't care what room you went into, the view was unbelievable.

In 1995 we moved to Mendocino because the Elk house and garden were getting too difficult for us to maintain. I was into my seventies and had major heart surgery. We were five miles from downtown Elk and just too isolated. Polly was working all day long at her office in Elk. I was sitting around the house, practicing and stuff. We both had gone through tragedies. It was high time for us to move on to a new place.

⁓

When Charlotte died, the very first thing that I did was to go to Friday evening services in one of the shuls in San Francisco. I said to myself, "Okay, Walter, you're leaning towards Judaism at this moment. Why don't you go to a Jewish service?" Which I did, three or four times, but I disliked the prayers and the services in Judaism almost as much as I had disliked all of the Christian services. I really didn't care for what the rabbis were saying on the pulpit.

When I first came here, the Mendocino community had a Jewish service and they had a rabbi. They had no home, no temple or synagogue. But I was accepted here, without exception, by everyone, and was bolstered by the communal feeling. That had never happened to me anyplace else. I had met intelligent ministers. I had met intelligent priests. But they just did not have the warmth and the identification that I needed. In Mendocino, Judaism was part of this Jewish community. Here there was that difference, of total identification with the clan, and that brought me back to Judaism. I will repeat, these are my people.

The Jewish community in Mendocino was community-oriented and that really gave me the impetus to be identified with my Judaism. They were mine and I was one of them. I joined the Mendocino Jewish Community about 12 years ago. The Judaism that I became active in here was mainly because of Rabbi Margaret Holub, our spiritual leader and the most amazing guide for Jewish literature and ritual. Margaret held the High Holiday services before the community bought the Shul in Caspar. She has a philosophical mind that I can attest to. Her Judaism is close to mine. Margaret showed so much compassion and respect for my life story. She understood that I had gone through a religious transition—not transformation—from one kind of Judaism to another. She is one of the people who urged me to write a book.

༉

Two years ago Polly and I decided to vacation in Europe. First we went to Paris, because people go to Paris. I was sitting in a hotel reading an article in the Paris edition of the *New York Herald Tribune*. "Look at this, Polly. There's a fight going on between a guy named Eichengrün, who invented aspirin, and the Bayer Company in Switzerland."

This Eichengrün survived Bergen-Belsen and lived for another three years before he died. I don't know his first name, however it's of great interest to me now. His children's children are still fighting the fight against Switzerland. The Bayer Company, of course, thinks that they have no rights to pursue this fortune.

From France, we went to Germany. Going into Germany was always a painful process for me. But I had decided, long before we left Mendocino for what would be my last trip to Germany, and specifically to Lippstadt, that I wanted to rid myself of some of the feelings of anger and find different ways to address a painful past. The best part was that I could content myself with the fact that 86 percent of the Germans who had lived during the Holocaust were not even alive anymore. There is a whole different generation now. So it would be an injustice to them to cast blame onto that generation of Germans. And beyond that, Germany has definitely changed for the better. There's no question in my mind that what they did was absolutely hateful and unspeakable. But it was time for me to do what I had to do to rid myself of these feelings that were a part of me. Time to bring myself some peace of mind.

Polly and I went to Lippstadt to possibly straighten the graveyard out one more time. The last time I visited the Jewish Cemetery, it had been in terrible shape. We decided that what we would do was to hire someone to clean up the cemetery, someone who would go there once a month to keep it in good condition. It wouldn't be very expensive to have this done. When we got there, none of that was necessary. The Jewish graveyard was in beautiful condition. We planted some flowers, said *Kaddish*, the Jewish prayer for the dead, and went on our way. It was the weekend and we never found out why the cemetery was maintained, except that the town government took care of the land. So perhaps my hope that the Germans have changed is true.

The Lippe River at Lippstadt

No one knew that I would visit Lippstadt, but the Jewish Cemetery had been cleaned up, totally. You could see the cemetery was cared for with love.

I will never know what happened, but that afternoon I bought a book in the small town museum about the history of Lippstadt's Jewish graveyard. That evening, sitting

Lippstadt City Hall

on my bed in the hotel that looked upon my old house 50 yards away, I read about the two soldiers, one English and one American, who came to Lippstadt and raised havoc because of the desecration of the Jewish graveyard. The story told how the two soldiers took the burgermeister out to the graveyard, telling him that he was so corrupt he had no business being the burgermeister, because he had not done one thing to help the Jewish cause. I remember what the Israeli soldier said to the burgermeister, "You had to kill everyone you saw who was Jewish. When you were finished with that, it wasn't enough, and you had to let all the people who died lie in an untended rotting graveyard." And I'd like to leave it there. I never knew the name of the Palestine Brigade soldier, but the museum literature of the 40s brought us some pride and I could finally say goodbye to my boyhood home.

～

When I first came to Mendocino, the Symphony of the Redwoods gave a concert at Sea Ranch, in Sonoma County. The concert was so miserable that I felt very distressed. Lovely people, like Marcia Sloane, worked so hard to make that concert happen, but it was a spiritless failure. The folks in the orchestra begged me to play and I agreed to, as long as I didn't have to play the rehearsal. Tyler Lincoln, the conductor, looked for the bassoon parts but couldn't find them. So I drove all the way up to Mendocino, got the music from Tyler's mother, then drove it back down to Sea Ranch. We played the concert and I thought, "God help me just to get through this." Coming from the San Francisco Symphony into that orchestra was really disheartening. I came home and said to Polly, "We have to do something. This group is struggling." First of all, we talked with Tyler, who had a background as a good pianist. He had a talent for conducting but the orchestra would become de-railed during a concert.

Symphony
of the Redwoods

So Polly and I sat in our house in Elk and discussed what might be done. We thought the best way to raise the standards of the local musicians was to sit them next to professionals. Then the question was, "Who could we get as a conductor?" Tyler was really a nice guy, but he just didn't have enough professional conducting experience. I said, "What if we go down to the Bay Area and talk to Edgar." Edgar Braun had studied with Pierre Monteux and ran the San Francisco Chamber Orchestra. I had known him for years and played as soloist with his orchestra in the Vivaldi and Mozart *Bassoon Concertos*. We asked Tyler what he thought of the idea. "It would be wonderful if you could hire Edgar Brown," said Tyler, "I'll help you all I can. I don't want to conduct anyway."

Polly and I drove down to see Edgar Braun, who was a lawyer in San Francisco's business district. Edgar was very interested in doing a music festival with us. We returned to

Mendocino Music Festival 1990

Mendocino and told Tyler what we had done, but he said, "I don't want to be involved in it at all." But Edgar Braun couldn't do it, so we had to look further. This was in 1986.

The first Mendocino Music Festival concert was in 1987. and the conductor was Allan Pollack. Both he and his wife, Susan Waterfall, had studied at Northwestern University near Chicago and at UC Berkeley. We started the Festival

Walter Green, Bassoon — Alan Pollack, conductor
Mendocino Music Festival 1990

and we were very successful. Mendocino community members were excited with the idea and many people volunteered to help. Mendocino Headlands State Park offered the use of land next to the Ford House in Mendocino as the location for a large tent.

We trained the local musicians first, people like Erik Van Dyke, who is a good player. He's totally devoted and one of many such musicians on the Mendocino Coast. I'm glad

Walter Green and colleagues, Mendocino Music Festival 1993

they're here and I'm glad I had a chance to know them both as musicians and as human beings. Then we brought in the professionals. Many of the professionals were the same people who played with the Marin Symphony. These are the people I got to come up here, together with some members of the San Francisco Symphony. I knew every one of those people. We also hired our first African-American player, a tympanist from the San Francisco Symphony named Elaine Jones. She was here for a number of years.

The Music Festival was here for two purposes. The first was to raise the quality of concerts played on the Mendocino

Walter Green conducting the Symphony of the Redwoods Orchestra 1996

Coast, which would gain public support, and the second was to get people inspired so they became members of the Symphony of the Redwoods Orchestra.

We built an organization which was excellent. My strength was in hiring musicians who were capable of putting on a good performance. The Festival got better and

Mendocino Music Festival tent

better, much to the great teaching ability of Allan Pollack. He is a superb teacher and conductor and did a very good job in every respect. My roles in the Festival were Personnel Manager and, of course, Principal Bassoonist. I also conducted some chamber music, including a Schönberg composition, something really modern and beautiful.

The acoustics in that tent were a nightmare. I hated playing there, because everything sounded real "thuddy"—thut thut thut—and I'd have to scrape reeds in a way that you would never get them to vibrate fully. It was nobody's fault. I suggested, maybe the second or third year, that we should try and get a hall, so that whatever we played was acoustically sound. But there is no appropriate hall in Mendocino and playing in that little theater in the Mendocino Art Center was very unsatisfactory. So unless a wealthy "angel" comes along, the Festival will have to make do with a tent.

I enjoyed the Festival, especially the first ten years, because there was a lot of positive interplay and camaraderie between Allan, Susan, and myself. I remember, after rehearsals, we used to love to go to the Sea Gull Restaurant for lunch. After performances Allan and I would go for quite a few beers, which was to soothe the hurt of inadequate rehearsals. I made up my mind to do the very best we could accomplish and I am very happy that Susan, Allan and I enjoyed such professionalism and joyful music making.

There is a lot for me to be proud of. In 1987 the Music Festival presented four orchestral concerts, with 56 musicians, and four chamber music concerts in a tent that seated 400 people. A fully staged opera was presented in 1989, a Young Musicians Scholarship Program began in 1992, and a Piano Series was added in 1995. Today the Festival has expanded to twelve evening concerts, with almost 100 musicians, plus jazz, blues, ethnic, and Big Band concerts. The new tent holds more than 800 people and more than 200 local volunteers help out.

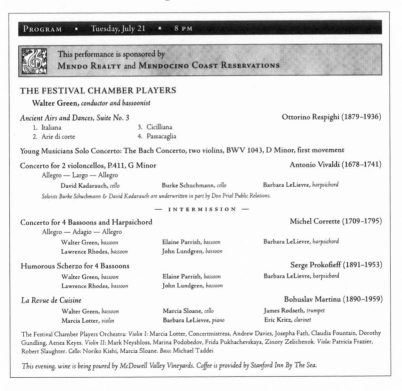

PROGRAM • Tuesday, July 21 • 8 PM

This performance is sponsored by
MENDO REALTY and MENDOCINO COAST RESERVATIONS

THE FESTIVAL CHAMBER PLAYERS
Walter Green, *conductor and bassoonist*

Ancient Airs and Dances, Suite No. 3   Ottorino Respighi (1879–1936)
  1. Italiana   3. Cicilliana
  2. Arie di corte   4. Passacaglia

Young Musicians Solo Concerto: The Bach Concerto, two violins, BWV 1043, D Minor, first movement

Concerto for 2 violoncellos, P.411, G Minor   Antonio Vivaldi (1678–1741)
  Allegro — Largo — Allegro
      David Kadarauch, *cello*   Burke Schuchmann, *cello*   Barbara LeLievre, *harpsichord*
      Soloists Burke Schuchmann & David Kadarauch are underwritten in part by Don Prial Public Relations.

— INTERMISSION —

Concerto for 4 Bassoons and Harpsichord   Michel Corrette (1709–1795)
  Allegro — Adagio — Allegro
      Walter Green, *bassoon*   Elaine Parrish, *bassoon*   Barbara LeLievre, *harpsichord*
      Lawrence Rhodes, *bassoon*   John Lundgren, *bassoon*

Humorous Scherzo for 4 Bassoons   Serge Prokofieff (1891–1953)
      Walter Green, *bassoon*   Elaine Parrish, *bassoon*   Barbara LeLievre, *harpsichord*
      Lawrence Rhodes, *bassoon*   John Lundgren, *bassoon*

La Revue de Cuisine   Bohuslav Martinu (1890–1959)
      Walter Green, *bassoon*   Marcia Sloane, *cello*   James Rodseth, *trumpet*
      Marcia Lotter, *violin*   Barbara LeLievre, *piano*   Eric Kritz, *clarinet*

The Festival Chamber Players Orchestra: *Violin I:* Marcia Lotter, Concertmistress, Andrew Davies, Josepha Fath, Claudia Fountain, Dorothy Gundling, Aenea Keyes. *Violin II:* Mark Neyshloss, Marina Podobedov, Frida Pukhachevskaya, Zinory Zelichenok. *Viola:* Patricia Frazier, Robert Slaughter. *Cello:* Noriko Kishi, Marcia Sloane. *Bass:* Michael Taddei.

This evening, wine is being poured by McDowell Valley Vineyards. Coffee is provided by Stanford Inn By The Sea.

Walter Green and Elaine Parrish 1997

On my 70th birthday party a few years ago my kids spoke and passed the accolades. It was sponsored by the Music Festival and it was supposed to be a fundraiser. One of my kids said, "You know how nervous I feel getting up in front of a hundred people and talking? It just gives me pleasure to know how wonderfully my dad came through those anxious moments," and he talked about it. So why did I do it? Because I so loved the bassoon and most of all, so loved music, not realizing then that I would continue to have the music in my life, but in time not the playing.

I wanted to find another facet of life, and I did. I was one of the three founders of the Festival and I worked very hard to bring up the quality of the Symphony of the Redwoods. I think that was terribly necessary, and I use the word "terribly"—you've got to start somewhere and we started somewhere. It was a wonderful experience to see the Festival flourishing during the first 16 years of its existence and its

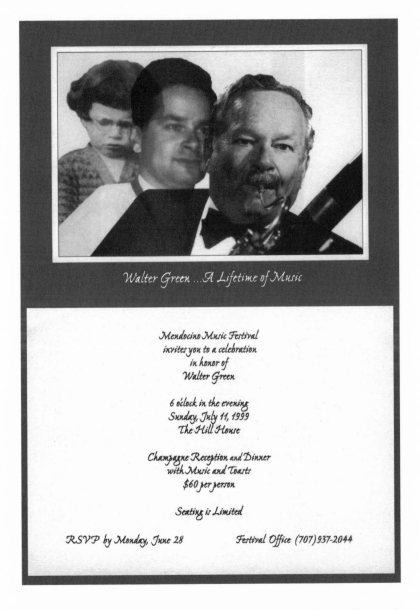

Walter Green ...A Lifetime of Music

Mendocino Music Festival
invites you to a celebration
in honor of
Walter Green

6 o'clock in the evening
Sunday, July 11, 1999
The Hill House

Champagne Reception and Dinner
with Music and Toasts
$60 per person

Seating is Limited

RSVP by Monday, June 28   Festival Office (707) 937-2044

coming to a beautiful fruition. This marked two bound-
aries for me: one, to start looking for something else, and
two, to feel my own inner self satisfied.

MENDOCINO

MUSIC FESTIVAL

<small>TWELFTH SEASON ▪ JULY 14 – 25, 1998</small>

(Art work by Marsha Mello)

৵

My health continued to be good, except for one more thing, which is Parkinson's Disease. In 1995 the Mendocino Music Festival was going to have a float in the Fourth of July Parade in Mendocino and I borrowed a truck to pull the float. As I drove the truck from Fort Bragg to Mendocino, I noticed that my hand was shaking. Not a strong tremor, but I couldn't get the shaking to stop. And it didn't stop. What my doctor thought of immediately was Parkinson's. I went to the most famous Parkinson specialist at Stanford University, who wasn't sure I really had the disease. She thought I had symptoms but not a full-blown kind.

The deterioration came very gradually, but the tremors worsened, so that I couldn't play the bassoon. That was really the biggest tragedy. I did everything I could to try to keep playing. I bought a new gadget, like a stand that I could put the bassoon on. You don't have to do anything except close the holes. I continued making reeds, at least until two years ago. I'm left-handed. The file would be in one hand, the reed in the other. I'd start filing away, then the damn thing would go weird. There was nothing I could do about it.

I took Sinemet, which has incredible disturbing side effects, like hallucinations. I worked with Ira Rosenberg, who does biofeedback. Ira has six computers, which he uses to measure EEGs. He taught me to meditate in certain ways, to calm my mind and body and center myself—then the tremor would stop. But when I thought about other things, my hand began to shake again.

I had to accept that I could never play music again, so I sold my bassoon. My buddy Jim in Indianapolis sold it for me. I was so sorry! I was sure heavy-hearted, but why should I torture myself? Should I look at the thing and not be able to pick it up? This comes from my heart—we will now have a moment of silent prayer.

Chapter 11
The Bassoon

First of all, the bassoon is not a strange-looking instrument—it is a weird-looking instrument! The place of the bassoon in the modern symphony orchestra is the same as the cello is in the string section. The bassoon plays the bass part in the wind or, you might even say, in the double-reed section. It is not analogous to a bass trombone. The purpose of a bass trombone is to play as softly as possible—that's a Richard Strauss quote. The composer used a bass trombone a lot. In general, it's oboe, contra bassoon, and bassoon as far as double reeds go. Except, again, for Richard Strauss, who uses an oboe *d'more* and oboe *d'caccia* in many of his operas and even in the *Symphony Domestica*. He also uses a *Heckelphone*, which is halfway between an oboe and a bassoon in pitch and sound.

The purpose of the bassoon is to add a bottom to the sound of the orchestra. Also, the bassoon is often talked about as the clown of the orchestra. Not the bassoonist, the bassoon. When you're playing something that is clownish or staccato sounding, you immediately think bassoon. A clarinet is much softer and an oboe is much more high-pitched. The oboe is also a double reed but much smaller and narrower. You can add a contra bassoon and that sounds like a bass trombone—in heat. The bassoon has three and a half octaves, which is very high for any woodwind instrument. No other instrument has that range.

No definitive evidence exists as to the invention of the bassoon. A Latin treatise of 1539 ascribes the instrument to

Canon Afranio, a priest in Ferrara, Italy, who played the *faggotto* and supposedly named it after himself. The Italian word for bassoon is *faggotto,* meaning "a bundle of sticks," which doesn't help explain the instrument's history. Hundreds, if not thousands, of different people modified the bassoon through the centuries, and still do. I added several keys to the instrument myself, because it was such an acoustic monstrosity. It has been very slow in its development as a modern instrument.

In the seventeenth century there were five varieties of bassoons, but only two are used today, the bassoon and the double or contra bassoon. Two types of bassoons are used today: the French Bassoon and the German Bassoon. In France they still play French bassoons. The French bassoon uses different fingering and has a smaller sound, with higher resonance and pitch, so it sounds different from the German instrument. Those instruments were used in France before the German bassoons were developed. The French bassoon had a smaller bore and sounds more like a saxophone than a bassoon. (Adolphe Sax came along in the mid-19th Century and invented the saxophone.)

When Herbert Von Karajan became the conductor of one of the French orchestras, he insisted that the bassoonists learn to play German bassoons because he didn't like the sound of the French bassoon. Years ago a principal bassoonist in the Boston Symphony played a French bassoon and was highly respected as a wonderful musician. The English for a while played French bassoons, but not any more. Today, except in France, only the German type of bassoons are used by professional musicians.

Sometimes composers wanted more of a bass sound. A composer had eight string basses standing there, but if he still wanted more bass sound he would add a tuba. If that still wasn't enough, he'd add a contra bassoon. The contra bassoon goes an octave lower than a bassoon, so we're really down there. Playing a contra bassoon was like having two frogs inside your lips and they go boing, boing, boing, because the vibration is so slow, to get that low sound.

In the early nineteenth century, a German bassoonist named Carl Almenraeder researched and described the acoustics of the 15-keyed bassoon. He also, together with J. A. Heckel, solved one of the instrument's most difficult problems. The bassoon is made out of rosewood or maple and has a conical bore, which is very important for the sound of the instrument. The tenor joint, which is made very narrow, joins the two parts of the bassoon. The tenor joint is lined with what Heckel called "cauchuck," a form of hard special india-rubber. So you have an instrument with one, two, three parts of wood and a fourth part, the tenor joint of the instrument, made of wood with a rubber lining. The other parts are not lined.

Water gets into the instrument, but the liquid doesn't touch the three other parts, the interior, of the instrument. The rubber lining kept the instrument from deteriorating because of moisture, but didn't change the tone, because the rubber was inserted in such a way that the circumference of the bore for the interior and exterior was the same. This was accomplished by putting the liner in the fourth part of the instrument, which is the part of the bassoon that gives it its tone quality. This technical change eventually made Heckel the foremost bassoon company in the world.

Today we are just breaking into a new market with bassoons. Hugo Fox played principal bassoon in the Chicago Symphony under Frederick Stock. After he quit playing, Fox studied how bassoons were made and was able to produce an instrument. At the beginning, about 1950 or 1952, they weren't very good. Then he began making better and better instruments and taught his son how to make bassoons. A few years ago I sold my Heckel and was using a Fox when

I stopped playing. Fox bassoons are American instruments, made in the Ohio River Valley.

When I was at Eastman, I was playing on those two bassoons that I'd bought in Austria while I was in the Army. Then I traded them in for an American-made instrument. Not so good, in fact it was terrible. But I was able to play it well enough to last me throughout my school years. I decided that I needed to find out why this instrument, which looked like a Heckel, didn't play like one. I wrote a letter to the Conn Instrument Company, who wrote me back a very nice letter. They told me that the wood Heckel used came from a secret source in Germany and that you couldn't get that wood anywhere else.

So then I wrote Heckel, where I had visited briefly at the end of the war. They replied, saying that they were always interested in having young people tell them what they felt was the deficiency of the instrument, and that the secret source of wood was not available to anyone else, which was why Conn or Fox couldn't make a bassoon like a Heckel. They thanked me again for having written to them, and, at the end of the letter, they said that their "secret" source of wood was in the Ohio River Valley. In fact, it was black maple. This is known as a hardy, vibrant wood. What they didn't say is that Heckel would take the wood from the Ohio River Valley, throw it up in a bin for 15 years, then get it down and look at it to see if there were any splits and splices. If the wood wasn't good, they'd throw it away or use it for kindling. American instrument makers, even if they got the right wood, wouldn't age it long enough.

An essential part of playing a bassoon is resonance. Resonance comes not only by the way the inside of the bore is shaped, but also how the wood is treated on its way to becoming a bassoon. Heckel found the answer to it. Fox finally found the wood, then he also found the answer. His bassoons are not better, but they are, for the most part, as good. They may even have a little more of a bass timbre or a soprano timbre, but it's the same instrument. A conductor couldn't tell the difference.

When you wrote to Heckel and asked him for an instrument, he would send a list of things for you to check off, on a piece of very formidable-looking paper. For everything that you wanted extra on the bassoon, as far as key work was concerned, he'd charge you extra. For every little thing that he put on there, he charged extra.

I bought a used Heckel bassoon through Professor Burghauser, which I played for approximately 20 years. Then it was time to get rid of the instrument, because it was getting old, and I sold it to a student. In those days a used Heckel bassoon was somewhere between $600 and $700. A new Heckel bassoon was over $1000. A new bassoon from Heckel today costs $36,000. If you want to order one, it takes approximately three years to get it. I don't know why. Who knows? If you want to order one from Fox, they probably have some in the factory.

The first time I went to the Heckel factory was when I was in the Army, on my way to Lippstadt to find out what had happened to my grandparents. I drove into the Heckel yard and they saw that my Jeep had G-2 bumper markings, which meant counter intelligence. An older man in the yard was so scared when he saw the bumper markings that he wouldn't talk to me! He was Wilhelm Heckel, and I never was able to talk to him, not at all.

I went to visit the Heckel factory again in the 1980s. There were three or four people there and Herr Gebhardt was the Heckel bassoon maker. They welcomed me with open arms and asked me to sign their guest book. I opened up the book and the first signature was that of Richard Strauss. I think, although I'm not sure, that the book also contained Wagner's signature. If you play bassoon and you happen to play the overture to *Tannhauser*, the bassoon part goes up to the high E, which didn't exist for the instrument in Wagner's time. But the composer wrote a high E in that overture, so if your bassoon didn't have the high E, you used your voice. Nowadays, kids just play that like it's nothing.

Gebhardt sat me down and we had a long conversation. I said, "What's that bassoon standing over there?" "Oh," he said, "That is the instrument we use to make all the other instruments from. It is the prototype." "Well," I said, "how'd you like to sell me the prototype?" "Absolutely not! I can't do that! We need the prototype." I asked him if I could play it. Gebhardt said, "Do you have some reeds with you?" I always carried reeds with me. It was the most beautiful instrument I've ever played. Oh my God, just unbelievable, absolutely beautiful! I drooled.

Then we had more *kaffee* and *kuchen*, and Gebhardt asked me, "Mr. Green, did you go to college?" We were speaking German most of the time. "Yes, I did," I answered. He said, "Did you ever live in Germany?" I said, "Yes, I did." "Were you born in Germany?" "Yes, I was." "Hmmmm," he said. There was a big silence between each one of his queries. "*Ja*, you know," he said, "ve had a very hard time during the war." I thought, "Yes, I'll bet you did!" And I said, "Well, how about selling me an instrument?" "*Ach*," he said, "Yes, how old are you, Mr. Green?" At the time I was 63 years old. "It will take three years to make the instrument, he said. "You still want it?" "Absolutely not." I replied. After that encounter I thought, "I'm going to buy a Fox bassoon and that's the right instrument for me, no matter what."

I didn't want to buy a Heckel bassoon, but I wanted to buy a couple of crooks, the vocals, and the pipes that go outside the instrument. They are very expensive. A crook nowadays would cost about $500. Mostly silver. If you get the right ones, it is like buying a new bassoon, because the crook makes the sound different. I had a choice of five or six, but I picked out two and played them on his proto-type. Gebhardt said, "You know, Mr. Green, you have been such a good customer of mine during the years that I'm going to not charge you for one of the crooks." He said that right after the conversation that implied that I was Jewish, without saying it. And I took his offer!

I had bought crooks from Heckel many times. When-ever you felt that your sound was lacking in some way, you bought a new crook. They last indefinitely but they lose some of their vibrancy. I don't know why, and there's re-ally no answer to that. Other people make crooks now, which are very good and used for different things. That high E I mentioned; you can get a crook that gets a High E. It suffers a little bit, and has vibration in the low register, but this is infinitesimal. It wouldn't be noticeable to you, but it would be to me.

A crook is seamed, and then rolled over. I have one with a patch, because there was a hole in the seam. I had a "leakey beakey." It cost me just as much to get the patch made as it would have to buy a new one. Different crooks are basi-cally the same instruments, but they are different lengths and different bores. The bore of the crook or the vocal is different inside, enough to make a huge difference in the sound.

So the crook and the way the pads are seated on the tone holes is of prime importance in playing the bassoon. My teacher used to say, "Hey, Walt! You gota hava da tools of da trade." I am sure there are some major bassoonists who use brands other than Fox or Heckel. This is not an Ameri-can invention. We took it to extremes, in a sense. Each one of these crooks has a number and a letter on it; different numbers for the different ways that the bore of the crook is tapered. I used to play CC1's and very rarely anything else. Two crooks may look exactly alike, but each will make an instrument sound totally different. It's like buying a Cadillac

Master musical instrument technician James Laslie

or a Rolls Royce—probably the Rolls Royce is better. Well, there's probably a bassoon that's better than another one and the crook will make it sound even better.

During the last year or so that I played, the Fox bassoon didn't do the job. I phoned my dear friend, Jim Laslie, colleague and genius of bassoon repair. Jim said, "I want to look at the bore. Send me the instrument," which I did. He wrote back, "The liner is coming loose from the wall of the instrument." You would think this happens a lot, but it doesn't. It was a rarity that the liner came loose on my instrument. The liner is glued in very snugly. Fox himself fixed it, at no cost. The rougher side of playing is repair and care.

I did not ask Gebhardt why it would take three years to get a Heckel bassoon, because we all knew that even if you were in the States and ordered an instrument, it would take three years. They were back-ordered that much because Heckel was almost the only instrument. This has totally changed now. Also, I hope the price is changing, although

Fox is getting more expensive. He also makes sailboats in his back yard, probably for use on the Ohio River.

The most important part of playing bassoon, in getting the sound, is the two reeds vibrating together when you blow into the instrument. You roll your lips over your teeth and make a kind of growling look and blow.

The bassoon uses a double reed, which is made out of a certain species of bamboo that comes from southern France, where farmers raise a lot of cane. It also grows in California, and more bassoonists are beginning to use California cane. Who manufactures the reeds? I do. Reeds are players' nightmares. All professional bassoonists make their own reeds. This is really an artist's work. It's nothing more than slicing stuff off a piece of cane, but it's not really the time that goes into it. I have about $4,000 worth of machinery for making reeds, so the job is a little easier now than it used to be, when we all made our reeds by hand. Now we can place a piece of cane into a machine that will taper and slice the reed to an almost-finished state.

You take a piece of wood and start slicing out the inside diameter. Then you put it on another machine and slice the outside of the reed. Then you fold the reed, very carefully so as not to break it. Then you tie it on the bottom. There's a certain way of tying it. You also hope that you don't shake too much while making reeds. That is one of the reasons I stopped playing.

So at a certain point you have the reed, but you've got to blow somewhere. So you need to shape a hole into it, and other things, to put it on the instrument. Then you open it up by cutting crosswise, and you have a reed. There are all kinds of things that go on, which get too technical.

And if you are playing in a major symphony orchestra, you must have more than one reed that plays well. You can blame all the mistakes on the reed, too, so that's a great way to ease your conscience. How long do they last? It de-

Basson reed

pends on the person, because the stuff that's going around in my mouth is different from what's going around in someone else's mouth. I'd say a week for one reed. You need one reed to play, but you must have five or ten more available. I've had reeds harden, when they start losing their buoyancy or their vibrancy, right in the middle of a concert.

When you buy the bamboo cane, you buy 50 pieces, 100 pieces, 500 pieces; it depends on how good you think the cane offered to you will be when used as bassoon cane. It's not expensive. It costs between $5 and $7 dollars a pound. You can get three good reeds a year from a pound of cane. I can't tell you how much a reed costs, except that my time is worth a lot less now than it was ten years ago. At least 60 percent, possibly more, of the practice session is reed making, both on the oboe and the bassoon.

In order to play the bassoon or the oboe, the reeds have to be wet. You soak them for ten minutes before you ever start playing. And you've got to have another one, maybe a couple of them, ready, soaking. You start playing when you first make them and then spend about five days either killing the thing or throwing it out a window or pushing it against a music stand. It's an ongoing headache all your life and there is no answer for it—not for me, anyway.

I learned to make reeds by watching other people make reeds. The reed lore just came into its own during the last fifteen years or so, when people wrote treatises on reed making. Before that, it was like father to son and on and on, which is the way I learned. Professors Ohlberger and Burghauser made their reeds a certain way. As soon as I got

Bamboo reed profiler

into the Eastman School, I made my reeds differently. They were a little bit narrower, by about a thirty-second of an inch.

You can buy reeds in a music store, but they cost as much as $15 each. Some people use commercial bassoon reeds, but not the great bassoonists. The great bassoonists all play on cane that they bought and tried out. As far as I'm concerned, there are no good commercial bassoon reeds. They also make plastic reeds, which last forever. They sound like hell. That's what kids would start on.

After you use the reed, you have to scrape it, because wood swells from the moisture in your mouth; then you have to scrape things off. You scrape until you think it's right and you try it and, no, it needs a little bit more off the tip and, whoops, the thing cracks! And you start all over again. Scraping is everything. Scraping constantly, with knives and files. Then someone invented a meter to tell the thickness of the upper blade and the lower blade. But basically, even if they work, at some point they will stop working. Not absolutely stop, but the thicker the reed is, the harder it is to play, because you have more resistance in the reed. As it gets thinner, it lessens the resistance because the vibration starts earlier. Having the thinnest workable reed is part of it.

Have you ever seen one piece of wood that is like another piece of wood, exactly? No, of course not. That's the whole story. I have screamed in frustration at reeds that didn't play, when it was going just beautifully, but then, instead of going whffffffff, it went whoooofff. There's no answer for it. You have to scrape the wood some more and hope that it will respond, but what can happen is that the thing flattens out on one note. The only kind of substance that seems to work for double reeds is this cane called *aronda donut*. And even that can only be a certain diameter. Apparently there is no other material.

—from Telemann *Sonata in F minor for Bassoon & Basso Continuo*

Chapter 12
Soloists

During the years I've played with and listened to many soloists. As for pianists, I talked about Artur Rubenstein, who was wonderful, one of the best. But really, there was only one pianist and that was Vladimir Horowitz. I never played with him, because he didn't play much with orchestras. Horowitz was a phenomenon. He had a nervous breakdown and was hospitalized in Switzerland for almost 30 years. Then he had a big comeback. He'd been practicing so long that his knuckles, which sometimes hit the piano, were bloody and bandaged.

Horowitz was featured on a special television program. It is hard to believe he was quite as friendly as he appeared in the television interviews. He wasn't. Charlotte and I went to some of his concerts in the Opera House in San Francisco and in Los Angeles. We just could not believe what that man was doing. It was unbelievable. He was a great musician, the greatest of the great! He was married to Toscanini's daughter.

Glenn Gould toured a lot and I played with him many times. The first time I saw him, he came in the door wearing a muffler, cut-off gloves, and a heavy overcoat. It was during the summer and the sun was out. He dressed like that, supposedly, so that he wouldn't infect himself with anyone's illness. He was a total *meshugane*. He astounded you. I asked our concertmaster, Frank Hauser, about one thing he did, "How come Gould used the music for the Bach *Concerto* and then did Schoenberg afterwards and he played it from memory. Why is that?" Hauser said, "No, no, no, what Gould was doing, while he was playing the Bach, he was studying the Schoenberg." Gould did this in performance. A total nutcase, but a highly original musician. He didn't relate to the musicians in the orchestra at all; they weren't even there. His Bach was certainly different. I don't know whether I liked it or didn't like it.

I played with William Kapell only once. During one of those summers when I was in the San Diego Symphony we played some chamber music at an orchestra member's home. Kapell played with us. He was one of the greats, absolutely, without a doubt. What a tragedy that he died so young. His recording of the Katchaturian *Concerto for Piano & Orchestra*—a piece of music I really don't like much—with the Boston Symphony and Serge Koussevitzky, is one of the great recorded performances.

Rudolf Serkin was one of the giants, great with a capital G. On every thing he ever did. And a nice man on top of it. There are four horns in the orchestra's horn section. First and third are high horns, second and fourth are low horns. There's a third horn solo in the Brahms *First Piano Concerto*. In Indianapolis the third horn player was practicing during intermission. This guy who looked like a janitor or something came across the stage and said, "Excuse me, I'd like to help you with this if I could. Would you mind, my name is Rudolf Serkin." He was like that. He was head of Curtis Institute for many years. My God, he was good.

Claudio Arrau played with us many times. Marvelous pianist. Gorgeous Beethoven player. Just a great musician and he related well to the orchestra members. By well I mean he said goodbye.

Robert Casadeseus was a wonderful pianist. The thing with Casadeseus was that every record collector made up his mind that the French could not play music. That was so ridiculous—like a similar bias against Zino Francescati.

Andre Watts and Walter Green 1984

Philippe Entremont was a young man when he played with us and all the older women loved him. He was both pianist and conductor. Entremont was a talented man, interesting, competent, but not great.

Leon Fleisher belongs in the field with Byron Janis, in that they both had carpal tunnel syndrome. Fleisher was a great pianist and a good conductor.

I should mention a few others, like Van Cliburn, who was a great pianist and very nice to people; Emil Gilels, a great pianist; and Alfred Brendel, who is very good and great with Schubert.

There were three pianists particularly (and many others, for that matter), that I wish I had played with. I thought Walter Gieseking's Debussy and his Mozart were just unbelievable. There was a certain tenderness about him that most pianists don't have. He was in the same league as Artur Schnabel, who was before my time, and was perhaps the greatest Beethoven interpreter of the twentieth century. Also Wilhelm Backhaus, who I personally think was a wonderful pianist with Romantic music.

Just as I was retiring from the San Francisco Symphony, Andre Watts played with us. His Brahms *Concertos* were out of this world. And the Tchaikovsky *Concerto* . . . ba ba ba boom! When he came in with those octaves, he spread his fingers . . . This guy played that like you've never heard.

༈

Jascha Heifetz was, I think, the greatest instrumental musician of the twentieth century. Oh yeah! He could do things that no one else could do. People who didn't understand him thought he was cold, but he wasn't cold. Anything but. They didn't get it, it just went right past them! He was so hot, you couldn't get to within a hundred feet of him.

The only other violinist who I think might equal Heifetz was Fritz Kreisler. I never played with him, of course, as he was much before my time. All we have of Kreisler are 78 rpm recordings. But I don't care whether I played with him or not, it was the experience of a lifetime to listen to that man play the violin.

My first job was as principal bassoonist of the beloved Utah Symphony and our soloist that evening for the Brahms *Violin Concerto* was Jascha Heifetz. I heard Heifetz warm up in his studio in back of the Tabernacle in Salt Lake City and the man played unbelievably. Of all the violinists, he was the best. There were people like Bronislav Huberman, Yehudi Menuhin, Nathan Milstein, and many others, but none of them matched Heifetz. He was the greatest musician I ever played with.

The closest thing to Heifetz (and maybe Kreisler), was Yehudi Menuhin. I played with him often. Also he conducted us. He was a very good conductor, an excellent musician. A lot of Mozart. A lot of stuff from the Baroque, but it didn't matter. Whatever he touched . . . I have a recording where he plays the Beethoven *Violin Concerto*, which just took my heart away. Always, always, always, he had something beautiful to say, both with his mouth and with every other part of his body. But most of all, with the violin. I had the highest respect for him. He had a heart of gold and was so musically intelligent. When he was about 30 years old, he developed carpal tunnel syndrome in his right hand and after that his recordings were not as good as they might have been. He tried to get help from Ravi Shankar and various physical therapists, but his condition never improved. However, incredible music making was always a part of the man and it was wonderful to play with him and I loved hearing him explain things about music because he was so intelligent.

Nathan Milstein (like Heifetz) was a student of Leopold Auer, who was not only a famous violinist, but the best violin teacher in the world. Milstein played the Brahms *Violin Concerto* with us in 1983. When we got through he said, "Anyone want a lesson, stick around." He gave the whole string section a lesson. It was just fantastic. Everybody stayed. Milstein had very few months to live, and he was going to give as much as he could. Changed my ideas about him. That set him apart from a lot of other soloists.

As a kid I used to love to listen to Joseph Szigeti playing with the New York Philharmonic with Bruno Walter conducting. They played lot of the popular violin concertos: Beethoven, Brahms, Mendelssohn, etc. But Szigeti played out of tune, which is something I can't get past. In those days, the kind of music you made was more important than how you tuned your instrument. And on AM radio, most people wouldn't know the difference anyway. But Szigeti should have tuned up with himself, not with the orchestra. I have a recording of his that is so badly out of tune, I can't believe it.

Tossi Spiakovsky was one of the very few violinists who played with a bow in the left hand and held the fiddle in the right.

I played with Zino Francescati at least a hundred times. It's a shame he was so little known in America, a victim of the anti-French bias that existed (and still exists), because he was more than a near-great. I think he was a fine, fine violinist. And businesslike. He came on stage and smiled at you and away we went and nobody fussed He was a wonderful violinist.

Arthur Grumiaux was also a wonderful violinist. His recordings of the Bach *Six Sonatas and Partitas for Solo Violin* are indescribable.

Isaac Stern. Let me give you an idea of what he was usually like. I was playing with the Indianapolis Orchestra. We were doing the Brahms *Violin Concerto*. He was standing up there in front of the maestro, Fabien Sevitsky. Stern stopped the orchestra, then stopped Sevitsky. Stern said, "What's that on the floor of the stage?" Sevitsky said, "It's a wire recorder." "Oh yeah!" exclaimed Stern and POW, he kicked the thing until it fell into a thousand pieces. That was Isaac Stern. He was not recording unless he got paid for it, although he didn't need to get paid more than he got paid, because he got paid an awful lot. He was a braggart, but a very fine violinist. Very wonderful. He made his debut in a film, *Intermezzo*. He was around for a long time.

Another time, in the San Francisco Symphony, Stern was soloist in the Brahms *Violin Concerto*. He was still a very young man at the time, very cocky. There was a passage that Stern wanted to take a little slower and Enrique Jordá wanted to take a little faster, and I didn't know whom the hell to follow. Finally I literally gave up and put the bassoon down. At the end of that part of the rehearsal I went to see Mr. Jordá. "Maestro Jordá," I said, "Whose tempo are we going to take? I don't know what to do." Now, you don't ever embarrass a conductor by saying it in an aggressive way, but you say, "Maestro, who do I have the honor of following?" Jordá said, "Just play it the way Mr. Stern wants."

Stern still wouldn't go along with it so we just kind of bumbled around until some compromise took place.

On the other hand, Charlotte and I were flying on a 747 to the wedding of our son, David, in Italy. A lady sitting next to me asked, "Are you Walter Green? My brother used to play in the Symphony. Do you know that Isaac Stern is in the First Class compartment?" I said, "Is that so?" She said, "Yes, why don't you go say hello to him." "No, he wants his privacy and I want mine," I said, "and I don't think it's the right thing to do." I could, I suppose, talk about musical ethics, but it's not necessary, because you learn very quickly. But the woman continued, "Oh, go up there and see Mr. Stern." I replied, "No, no." Then Charlotte started in, "Walter, you know him. You've played with him hundreds of times."

So I walked up to the first-class compartment and as I drew the curtain back the stewardess said, "You can't come in here." I said, "I'm on my way to see Mr. Stern." "Oh, you know him?" I said, "Yes." And I went up to Isaac and said, "How are things in New York?" because we were heading New York way. Stern said, "Oh, my goodness. What's the San Francisco Symphony doing here?" I sat down with him and we started talking. Stern said, "You know, my beard is really rough. I just played Tokyo last night and I've got to play a recital in Carnegie tonight." He was like that. Just on and on and on. I said, "Well, I'm sorry you feel tired." He answered, "Not tired. I need a razor. I don't have a razor with me." I said, "Can I lend you my razor?" He said, "Would you be so kind?" I said, "Sure, I'll go back and get it. It's an electric razor, if that's all right with you."

So I got my razor and gave it to him. He said, "Thank you, that's very kind of you." I said, "I'll wait for you while you shave and you can give it to me then." He said, "No, no, you go back to your seat. I'll bring it to you there." Well, after he finished, he walked through the whole damn plane, one side to the other, and when he came to our seat, he rushed right over to Charlotte and said, "Mrs. Green, I want you to know that I've admired your husband for a long time and he's wonderful and I wish you the very best at the wedding of your beloved son." Charlotte said, "Well, thank you." I said, "It's wonderful to see you. See you soon," and Stern walked back to the first-class compartment.

Even though he recognized me immediately, I don't know if it was as the San Francisco Symphony's principal bassoonist or because I was at that time Chairman of the Orchestra Committee. It's a nice, though unimportant story, but Stern was most gracious, in contrast to some earlier times when I had observed him.

ॐ

Not only did I perform with soloists, but I also was a soloist myself through the years. I played the two Mozart *Concertos* and also four Vivaldi *Concertos*. Vivaldi, the famous Italian Baroque composer, worked as a teacher in a girls' school. Whenever somebody graduated, he'd write her a concerto. He wrote over 36 bassoon concertos. Can you believe that? I remember when they came on microfilm to the Eastman School's Sibley Library. My teacher, Mr. Pezzi, and I looked through these concertos. It was just absolutely thrilling to see that much music for bassoon.

I've mentioned various pieces of music that contain great bassoon solos and one that I enjoyed very much was Prokofiev's *Peter and the Wolf*. The music is scored for quite a small orchestra and one instrument represents each character in the story. I loved playing the bassoon's role, the part of Grandpa. But I also stood in front of the orchestra to narrate the story.

We did four Children's Concerts and the conductor was Verne Sellen, who knew me from the Cazadero Music Camp. He asked me to narrate the Prokofiev. At the end, as I came off stage, Kurt Herbert Adler walked by. I was coughing,

219

after having spoken the words, and Adler said, "Diaphragm, diaphragm! You must sing with the diaphragm." Those were the only times that I stood in front of the orchestra to talk, except when I retired.

We did two other narrated works, Benjamin Britten's *Young Peoples Guide to the Orchestra*, and Aaron Copland's *A Lincoln Portrait*. I can't remember who narrated the Britten, but I'll never forget the two people who spoke *A Lincoln Portrait*. One was the famous American poet, Carl Sandburg; the second was Martin Luther King's wife, Coretta Scott King. Oh, she was wonderful. She had us in tears.

—from Vivaldi *Concerto for Bassoon in F major*

Chapter 13
Conductors

I love talking about conductors, because I think conductors are a question mark. I don't understand conductors. I don't understand the way they bring music out of an orchestra, because there are so many negatives involved between orchestra and management. They're an enigma to me.

What is it about conductors? What is it that is so magical about conductors? Well, the conductor gets up there and out of this little baton comes a whole Beethoven Symphony. If that isn't magic, all of its own, and the power that comes with it, then I don't know what is. That's why conductors are there and, beyond that, they put all this play into motion.

When we talk about the value of a conductor we talk about a man with a great repertoire and a phenomenal memory. For the most part, anyone who conducts a major symphony orchestra must be quite good and some of are absolutely great. But great conductors are the vast minority, few and far between. I get this information from myself and from what I've experienced over many years.

All the years that I was in symphony orchestras, every year we played all nine Beethoven Symphonies, and with a great conductor, they become even more potent and beautiful. There are very few great conductors, very few, and the nincompoops that are there shouldn't be conducting. But this never happened in the opera, because there was always something new at the opera. Even in *La Bohème*, there's always something new. Absolutely. Or in *Aida*, there's always something that can go wrong, even after you perform it a hundred times. It's wonderful. First of all, it's some of the most inspired music I've ever heard. Second, nobody writes a tune like Verdi and third, I totally love chamber music and opera. Listen to *Suor Angelica*. Nobody ever really tries to divide their mind up and listen to Puccini's orchestration, which I think is astounding. He was 50 years ahead of his time in that one opera.

I conducted a little bit and I fell into the conductor's trap. The strain is enormous. I conducted four partial symphony concerts and also five operas in Mendocino. The opera was my joy here. That was Opera Fresca with Clare Barca. Doing the opera was wonderful, but doing the symphony concerts and rehearsing within the guidelines of the time allowed for rehearsal made me so angry. Also, that somebody would interrupt my conducting without realizing what was happening. So I thought, "Well, I guess these guys have to be partially forgiven." They made me "eat crow" and like it.

The best conductor I ever performed under? I don't know, there's such a difference between "best" and "favorite." Certainly the man who changed music most in this country and in Europe was Arturo Toscanini. I never performed with him, but it didn't matter. At Rockefeller Center they opened a studio just for the NBC orchestra and dubbed it Studio 8H. It was a musical myth. The acoustics were absolutely awful. When you hear the recordings now there is no resonance. None of it mattered when it came to the way he balanced and prepared an orchestra. It was beyond belief. And I have the proof here. Watch him conduct Verdi's *La Forza del Destino* on videotape. It's electrifying. It's beyond that.

And Toscanini was a very nice, decent human being. I like what he did to get the Israel Philharmonic started, where the concertmaster was Bronislav Huberman. I liked the way he stood up for freedom. He really did. He stuck his neck out. He got beaten up on the street one day in Italy, under Mussolini, while he was walking to a rehearsal. And talk about the way he conducted Puccini's operas—it was never done again like that.

Paul Renzi told me some interesting thing about Toscanini, from the years that he was in the NBC Orchestra. Toscanini would scream at the players. He'd just bawl you out if something was wrong until you were mincemeat, but one second later it was over. He never talked about it again. Never called you into his room. It was finished, right then. That was it. Everybody got a Christmas present, even if they were Jewish. He didn't bear any grudges. There was only one man fired from the NBC Orchestra with Toscanini in 17 years. He got the absolute best out of everybody. And it wasn't the best orchestra in the world, but when he conducted it, I felt, for the amount of technique that they possessed in those days, which is a long time ago now, that technique was outstanding. If only those recordings could have been Carnegie Hall instead of Studio 8H.

Toscanini had such a feeling of honorableness, if there is such a word. When he was an old man, in his eighties, they were going to make another recording of the Beethoven *Ninth*. At one of the rehearsals, he got the chorus, the soloists and the orchestra together—and that's a big togetherness—and he conducted for five minutes, then screamed at himself, "Toscanini lousy, no good today, another day." And he walked out. All the musicians were paid for a three-hour call, even though Toscanini refused to conduct any longer. That was it. He wouldn't do it unless it was good. Those kinds of things influenced me a great deal. There's a Toscanini joke, which made more sense when concerts were transmitted over telephone lines: Two birds are sitting on a telephone wire. One looks at the other and says, "Hmmm, it's the NBC Symphony. I can tell by Toscanini's tempo."

Bruno Walter. I understand that in his younger days he was a holy terror. But one of his first cellists had a heart attack and died right on stage and Walter changed. I have this wonderful rehearsal recording of the Mozart *Symphony Number 38*. That's the one without the minuet and Bruno Walter was rehearsing a pickup orchestra. You could tell he was really a very thoughtful, kind man; but it took some tragedy like that to cause the change. Bruno Walter was a great conductor, if for no other reason than that he brought the Mahler symphonies to the consciousness of the listening public. When I played with him in one set of concerts we did Mozart's *Don Giovanni Overture*, then we played the Mozart *Linz Symphony* and we ended with the Bruckner *4th Symphony*, the "Romantic." I'll tell you, there was so much music coming out of that wonderful man and his devotion to Bruckner, Mahler, and Mozart. Bruckner symphonies are repetitious at times but certainly are far from boring, as many critics seem to think. Walter was outstanding, an absolutely great, great conductor and a wonderful human being. I think Arturo Toscanini and Bruno Walter are the two great conductors of the twentieth century. When I hear the Beethoven symphonies conducted by Bruno Walter, or anything in the romantic style conducted by him, I see a man of great inner passion and artistry. He was a very spiritual man. He was Jewish, but he converted early on. I've never heard Mozart performed better.

Sir Thomas Beecham. Absolutely one of the greats, absolutely superb. I've never heard anything of his that wasn't beautiful. Just amazing. I heard him conduct the Buffalo Philharmonic when I was going to Eastman and he said, "I cannot play any more encores, because we're going to see the Niagara Falls, in the moonlight." And he made his characteristic puckering sound with his lips. Beecham came to us many times. He sat out World War II in Seattle. When he went back to England and put the Royal Philharmonic together, for the first concert, as he walked down the center aisle, no one applauded, because he'd left the United Kingdom during the War. He went up on the stage, stood there, then bowed his head and said, "We'll now have a moment of silent prayer." A great sense of humor. He was more than competent. He conducted Richard Strauss as good as anyone else. His Mozart was just splendid. He conducted Beethoven very, very well. Whatever he did with nineteenth century music, including Frederick Delius, who was an unpopular composer, was done well. I went on tour one year with the St. Louis Symphonietta, which was made up of great players from all the Midwestern orchestras. A couple of times Beecham came to us. He had the gout, and for one afternoon performance he arrived 30 minutes late.

I've known people who say, "Well, I don't listen much to Beecham." I listen to Beecham a lot. He has a lot to say to me. I have this videotape where he's conducting. He describes how he rehearses and says, "I say, let's start the symphony, and we start the symphony and . . . Well, they know that. They've played the music so often, with so many conductors, so I put that aside. That's a good enough rehearsal for the concert this evening." So he goes through the rehearsal in 25 minutes, then lets them go. It is such a joy and gladness, that this conductor has seen tedium in his musicians, that he gets a hell of a concert performance. This didn't happen once, it happened often, because he avoided the tedium. Beecham talked a lot about the boredom of the orchestra and he joked, horsed around. It was his orchestra, the Royal Philharmonic, which he created with his own money, from Beecham's Pills. Beecham knew how to treat an orchestra.

He was a fine conductor and a marvelous gentleman and he had a very high standard. When he was guest conductor in San Francisco he had his 26-year-old wife with him. He was in his eighties at this point. "How was that, my dear?" "Just ducky." Twenty measures later, "How was this, my dear?" "Just ducky, my dear." They kept saying "ducky."

Leopold Stokowski. There was only one "Stokey." He had the ability to make you play with a tone that was pure gold and if you can tell me how that works, I wouldn't understand it. And it wasn't only the Philadelphia Orchestra strings, the 32 players. The point is that Eugene Ormandy continued that sound, although he certainly was not a great conductor, far from it, but he did get that sound out of the Philadelphia Orchestra. Stokowski somehow transferred something from him to you that cannot be described. It was just something that made the music absolutely sing, no matter what he did, and he did a lot of no-nos. I have a recording of the Tchaikovsky *Fourth Symphony* that is almost over before it starts. He did a lot of Bach transcriptions, which are just marvelous. It's not Bach, but it's marvelous. He was an absolutely great conductor. He made a lot of recordings with many different orchestras and he knew how to get sound out of any orchestra. We had a guy in the orchestra who had a shirt on with cowboy buttons and Stokowski didn't like him. I once heard Stokowski say to him, "You, cowboy, come here."

Eugene Ormandy. He had a very good beat and he always came out with good recordings. He had a beat that preceded the baton like vanilla pudding, meaning that the baton dragged, like he could barely get it through. That's why his performances were so wonderful.

Sir John Barbirolli. A great conductor. I'll never forget when he conducted the Beethoven *Fifth*. "Da Da Da Dum," and he took the baton and hit his chest with it to get the orchestra to stop playing at the end of the first phrase. You could have sliced an onion. When he took over the New York Philharmonic from Toscanini, everybody gave him a hard time. He never made it big in the United States, but as far as I'm concerned he was great and a real gentleman. Barbirolli conducted a lot of Elgar, but whenever he did a classical piece or a romantic piece he was absolutely first rate. His wife, Evelyn Rothwell, was a wonderful virtuoso oboist.

Wilhelm Furtwängler. I never played with him, but he certainly must be counted as one of the great conductors. He conducted the Berlin Philharmonic for about 40 years and when he left Herbert Von Karajan took his place as the main conductor of the orchestra.

Dmitri Mitropoulos. Before my time. He was a saint of a man. I think he was a good conductor, very good but not great, but he did modern music very well, especially the first performance and radio broadcast of *Wozzeck* by Alban Berg.

Pablo Casals. I was most unhappy with Casals and so was the rest of the orchestra because he championed for ten minutes the musicianship of Enrique Jordá. He did his oratorio, *El Pesebre*, but the orchestra didn't like it. But we were in such awe of him as a musician, as a *mensch*, as a cellist beyond belief. He was touring with his oratorio. Playing it and hearing his concepts of music was just wonderful. When he worked at the Marlboro Music Festival It was first rate. It was great competition for the Boston Symphony, which played at Tanglewood. Casals was very old but still had energy to conduct such a large musical work. He went all over the country with *El Pesebre* and played it with all kinds of different orchestras. Made a job out of it for himself. In San Francisco he conducted the oratorio with the San Francisco Symphony. The chorus was usually made up partially from the San Francisco Opera and partially the Stanford University Chorus and outfits like that and they put it together pretty fast. But we were all disappointed in Casals, because he'd been our everything—historically, politically, musically—in every which way he excelled. He did the *El Pesebre* and then he gave a speech about how wonderful Enrique Jordá was as a conductor and we all felt totally cheated.

Igor Stravinsky. He was not a good conductor. Technically he just didn't know as much as he should have known. He could not even do great performances of his own music. There is a recording on Columbia of *The Rite of Spring* with the composer conducting the New York Philhar-

Igor Stravinsky 1970
A signed photograph given to Walter Green

monic. There are some very complicated rhythms at the end of the piece, one after another. I think Stravinsky could have written the thing in 4/4 but he was going to do it the way he was going to do it because it makes for these stress-filled rhythms. In the recording, the orchestra becomes lost toward the end of the piece and nobody knew where they were supposed to be. Yet the recording was released.

Artur Rodzinski. Talk about weird. When he conducted the Cleveland Orchestra he had to have his wife nearby. She had a whip and he had her whip him before he went on stage, and where in hell have you ever heard such a thing? People backstage saw what happened. He was a damn good conductor. His Sibelius *Fifth* was one of the great recordings.

Istvan Kertesz. He conducted us for two sets of concerts. We did the Bartók *Concerto for Orchestra*, which was wonderful to do with a Hungarian. He certainly knew the piece. It was the first time I had ever played it and there is one very difficult three-bassoon solo part. Maestro Kertesz died swimming in the Mediterranean in Israel and his death was a great tragedy. He was already one of the greats, and he had a great future.

228

Thomas Schippers. Died early, very good conductor. Might have been great.

Paul Kletzki. A very good, warmhearted conductor from Israel. Lovely man.

Karl Münchinger. I played with him at Stanford University, where we did *Cosi Fan Tutte*. I played principal bassoon with the Stuttgart Chamber Players. A good solid musician.

Tullio Serafin. He did the opera with us. He made some great operatic recordings with the La Scala Opera.

Guiseppe Patanè. A first rate opera conductor. He was in the same class as Molinari-Pradelli. He came from a family of good conductors.

Mstislav Rostropovich. He conducted Tchaikovsky's *The Queen of Spades* for the San Francisco Opera. As we came out of the opera house he paid me a great compliment. He looked at me, put his arms around me, gave me a Russian squeeze that I didn't recover from for five days, a real bear hug, and said, "This is the man who plays with such a beautiful tone." And I thought, "Boy, I've had it all now." A couple of years later he came back and did Tchaikovsky's *Eugen Onegin*. Kurt Herbert Adler called me in and Rostropovich said, "Ah, here comes my honest musician. A real honest musician! Isn't he?" All Adler could say was, "Eh!"

Julius Rudel. I had such an argument with him one time. It's not important, these things come up that are silly and you make such a big deal of them and 20 years later you come back and visit that scene and think, "Why the hell was all that?" Julie Rudel is a very good conductor.

Aaron Copland. A very good conductor, a magician where his own music is concerned, but that's all he usually performed. For six years the San Francisco Symphony played a series called Music Viva, which was modern music that had not been played previously. Copland was our conductor and he was very successful. He was a tall man who towered over us, particularly from the conductor's podium. I love his music.

Lukas Foss. Good composer, good but not a great conductor.

Morton Gould. Good with his own music, some of which is very interesting.

Andre Kostelanetz. Well, you know, he was good for light fluff. He conducted a lot in San Francisco, for the Winter Pops concerts.

Leonard Slatkin. Very good with American music. He is a good conductor, not great, but a very nice man.

Felix Slatkin. Another good journeyman conductor.

Robert Shaw. A magician with choruses. Absolutely wonderful. If he'd never done anything else he'd still be great. As an orchestral conductor he was good, but not great.

André Previn. I think he is on the verge of becoming a great conductor. He does especially well with recorded music. First rate. Hopefully he'll be great some day, because he has a lot to offer.

Wolfgang Sawallisch. A great, triple-great conductor of the Philadelphia Orchestra.

Zubin Mehta. A great musician, period.

Ricardo Muti. He was so good looking, a gorgeous hunk of man. He did a beautiful Schoenberg *Verklarte Nacht* in San Francisco.

Carlo Giulini. He conducted everything too slow. I went to sleep.

Bernard Haitink. A great conductor. First rate, superb, and a very nice man. I played a two-week series of concerts with him and I went on stage with 104° temperature and played the concert. I was soaking afterwards.

Lorin Maazel. He started conducting when he was 12 years old. Obviously a very good conductor, but cold as can be. When I played the Sibelius *Fifth Symphony* with him, a symphony you can emote with warmth and wonder, it was so cold that you could have chilled an iceberg. I must have missed something, because I've seen him on television and he's sounded and looked very good.

Claudio Abado. He never conducted us, but I can tell you from all that I've heard of him, and I've seen some television of him conducting the Berlin Orchestra, some Wagner performances, that he is a great conductor.

Daniel Barenboim. There's a whole connected story here. He was married to Jacqueline Du Pré. When she walked on stage, all the men in the orchestra just died a hundred times, because she was so beautiful. And she played so magnificently that when I hear a recording of hers, there isn't any other cellist who could touch her. Barenboim is a very good conductor and a marvelous pianist.

Sir Charles Mackerras. He is unknown except for recordings. He is first rate, absolutely wonderful. He did recordings with the Czech Philharmonic that are phenomenal. I've talked with a few musicians who have played with Mackerras, and they all really respect him.

Sir Georg Solti. He was a great conductor, there's no question, but there was something about him that I didn't like. I never could warm up to the guy. The only time I played with him was in two weekly concerts. He was very young then, but one could sense his enormous talent. It showed itself later on when he started doing Wagner's *Ring*. That is when his talent really came to the foreground.

Neeme Järvi. My good friend, Leonid Gesin, used to play viola in the Leningrad Orchestra before he joined the San Francisco Symphony. Leonid and Neeme Järvi were classmates at the conservatory in Leningrad. Neeme conducted here and I met him at Leonid's house. He told me that I was a great bassoonist, which, of course, was music to my ears.

Antal Dorati. One of my favorites, a superb musician who conducted us a few times. He was one of those guys who caused trouble, but since he was only a guest conductor it didn't really come out. He's a journeyman. It's all there when he gives a downbeat, you know exactly where the downbeat stops, and where the second beat starts. Totally, completely professional.

Benjamin Britten. A marvelous musician. Triple AAA. His operas are wonderful, to play and to listen to. He has no peers. The recording of him conducting his great *War Requiem* is astounding.

Sir Simon Rattle. He may turn out to be one of the very best. He has conducted the greatest recording ever made of Mahler's *Fifth Symphony*.

Leonard Bernstein. I only played one concert with him, in New York. He was a great conductor. That's all there is to it. There's no question in my mind, especially in the last few years. He did a Mahler *Ninth Symphony* in Vienna with the Vienna Philharmonic and I had the privilege of attending both the rehearsal and the concert. During the rehearsal Bernstein started yelling at the orchestra, that they should not have put the bust of Mahler in the basement because he was Jewish. "No wonder you aren't playing this correctly, you don't understand Mahler, you don't know Mahler, and you insult Mahler, even after his death." He totally flipped, something he never did. And after it was over, it was over. Fabulous musician. You couldn't say that he was a great conductor without saying he was also a great composer. Or that he wrote the greatest musical ever written for Broadway, *West Side Story*. *The Age of Anxiety* is wonderful. The *Kaddish Symphony* is marvelous. The *Mass* is a gigantic composition.

James Levine. From the word go, he is an absolutely great conductor. This man totally transformed the Metropolitan Opera orchestra, singers, and management. That was a sloppy orchestra for many years. When he left recently to become the conductor of the Boston Symphony, the Metropolitan lost a great artist and conductor.

Michael Tilson Thomas. He was very nice. He was so very young. He had the Buffalo Philharmonic and he had a lot of guest shots. He was a guest conductor at the Hollywood Bowl and other places and people liked him. I like him. He's one of those guys of the new breed who really know how to conduct technically. I'm very impressed by his music making, because not only is he knowledgeable, he has a great sense of showmanship. I don't know what he's like as a person, although I had a chat with him once and he seems quite congenial and down to earth.

Kurt Masur. He conducted my very last performance as principal bassoonist with the San Francisco Symphony. We were playing the Beethoven *Ninth*. Masur is one of the older breeds, in his late seventies. Every time I played with him, I got a thrill out of it. He could be a tough one, but he didn't do that as a guest conductor. But I've heard from people who played in the New York Philharmonic, where he was permanent conductor, that he was tough. He was the best of the lot. No question about it. He's been an opera conductor, so he knows his stuff.

I have nothing but praise for the man. Partly because, being the assistant principal, and because it was my last concert, Masur said I should play first, principal bassoon, on the Beethoven *Ninth*. Afterward, I was made to stand up and come in front of the orchestra and take several bows from the audience. There was a party for me backstage. Off-stage were four bassoonists who played a *tuche*, a fanfare, for my retirement. They honored me that whole last week. They wanted me to speak, so I said to the orchestra, "What did I learn in those 27 years? What I really learned was that all music is surrounded by silence." And it really is. It's very important to know how long those silences last before you come in with whatever you're going to play. And the great conductors, that's the one thing they all have in common— how to respect and honor and play the silences.

We were just talking about the Beethoven *Ninth Symphony*. Within the music itself the eighth note only gets an eighth of a beat, not a quarter beat, just the time of an eighth. And there is a silence and then comes the next eighth note, and so on. I am thinking right now about the last movement, but I could be talking about all music. All music is surrounded by silence.

—from Beethoven *Trio in G major for Flute, Bassoon and Piano*

Chapter 14
Reflections on Music & Family

I want to say something about my relationship to music. It isn't the difficulty of playing an instrument, but it's the difficulty of playing an instrument as well as you can play, and that was always a hard task. Just because you're a professional isn't the answer. Music and musicians are very different today than what they were when you and I were young. Things have changed. The technical parts of performances make the instrument, that is, the symphony orchestra, the opera orchestra, a different "cup of tea" than it was back then. I remember when the Boston Symphony was recording Ravel's *Second Daphnis and Chloe Suite*, with Serge Koussevitzky conducting. The principal flutist, George Laurent, had a big solo in this music and he goofed up in one of the solos. They did another take of it. When the recording was published, the record company chose to use the first take, with the mistake in it. That was not such a big deal. When the Vienna Philharmonic played under Bruno Walter or Toscanini before the Hitler years, if somebody made a mistake it wasn't so important. If somebody makes a mistake today, it becomes a big deal immediately.

The technical perfection of the American orchestras today is just amazing. What has happened is that musicians, in learning to play music, have opted to play as perfectly, physically, as possible. Not necessarily as beautifully. That's something else and it's from another part of the last century. So we get these wonderful players, who play with less heart, but are more technically perfect.

I've tried to keep the attitude toward music, "Let me sing at all times." I've tried to keep that in my consciousness. If I don't sing, I'm not playing correctly. If I make a mistake, it's too bad, and I'm sorry, but it isn't that important, within reason. The two elements—perfection and beauty—that are the most elusive are the most desirable to be preserved. In order to play like that—and I've found this out by being a pro—you have to play a very thin edge. To get perfection is the real goal and it takes a lot of guts to play like that. It's not easy. It sounds more like a romance to the heart. But Renzi knew how to do it. Absolutely! Mark Lifshey knew how to do it. Walter Green knew how to do it, and I'm not being overbearing about how good I was.

When I go to Symphony concerts in San Francisco, with Michael Tilson Thomas conducting, he does a magnificent job with the orchestra. Just wonderful. Technically, it's a greater orchestra than it's ever been. But what has happened to the music? The conductor wants physical perfection, sure, but he really should be talking about phrasing and thin edges.

꒰꒱

I do love this area, especially Mendocino, and the joy it's given me to make music here. I love Mendocino and I will say it again and again. Development has changed it to a certain extent, sometimes not for the best, but Mendocino is still a most beautiful and wonderful place, and I'm grateful to live here.

To make music in any way possible is the most impossible and possible dream. And I still have that dream. I hope I have more time left to pursue music in some way. I'm not sure what that way is. It needs to come as a divine inspiration, and I say that with tongue in cheek. I need to work on myself, most of all, and to bring music to as many people as possible.

Fourteen years ago I went to the Mendocino County Fair in Boonville. Sean Donovan was sitting there, trying to talk people into supporting a public radio station before there was one. We became acquainted and he asked me, "Would you like to do a classical music program? I think you would be good at it." "Yes," I answered, "I would." So on the very first broadcast of KZYX I programmed *The Wonderous World of Music* and this has continued for 13 years. I love KZYX, and I can do no wrong there. Plus I have my assistant, Gordon Black, who fills in when I can't make it. I like the liberal attitude that exists at KZYX and I love that the people who work there hug each other, for good reason. Most of them are volunteers and are all in this together, trying to make a go of it, trying to do a really good job.

Broadcasting the beauty of music at KZYX (Photo by Miel Newstead)

❧

This is about my children. Nancy is a most warm human being and she loves her daddy. She lives in San Francisco and is a hair stylist. My oldest son, David, lives in Italy, near Lago Maggiore, with his son, Andrew, who is 21 and attends college in Milan. David is a highly intelligent young man, a loving son and a wonderful father. He is a linguist and teaches English to Italian students. My youngest son, Peter, is a warmhearted, wonderful young man, married to a wonderful, warmhearted young woman, Elise. They live in San Francisco and have a son named Nathan, who is the cutest thing I've ever seen. Peter is a buyer for a biomedical company.

None of the three kids became musicians. They saw the seamy side of music backstage and they shied away from it. Nancy has a lovely voice. David played very good violin when he was a youngster. Peter never sang or played anything, but one day, when he was in his teens, he was washing the dishes and I heard him sing "tim tim da ti da tim tum," which I realized was Bach's *Second Brandenburg Concerto*. He had been sneaking it by us. I still have a recording that Charlotte made for her high school graduation, playing the Second Movement of Beethoven's *Appassionata Sonata*. Although it wasn't professional, it was a damned good attempt at being a very good musician.

I spend a lot of time going through pictures and stuff of the kids and I never know where to start or where to stop. It's just so hard, because I want to praise them all for having fulfilled my dreams of them. And they are fulfilled and so are Charlotte's desires for her children. There really isn't much more to say about the kids, because it is their own lives that highlight them.

ॐ

I have been married to two wonderful women and have had two marriages of such quality and joy that this has been a miracle all in itself!

꒱

Finally about myself. I'm a musician by profession and that has been a blessing in my life. My life has been difficult in terms of what was demanded of me as a musician and as an artist, but it's been worth every moment. Even though I've talked about run-ins with conductors and other negative encounters, all these men are nothing short of fabulous when you think of what they must keep in their heads and bring out from musicians. Someone once asked me, "What really happens to you when you play and when the other people play? What is the process?" The process is magic, absolute and pure magic. Something happens between the conductor and the player and that indefinable something is what makes the magic.

I'm glad I've had a chance, over a lifetime, to experience this magic and I'd love to share it with all of you if I could, except I can't. That's why it's magic! I've so enjoyed the weeks of work, months of work, years of work, and the work that has been put in by all of us. I'm just glad that the Almighty has given me a chance to deeply experience this work. So if I could say one thing about Walter Green, it is that I hope I've contributed to the magic as much as my fellow musicians have, both conductors and players. And I thank them for that.

Magic doesn't always happen, of course. You can't guarantee it. Magic comes of its own volition. But when that magic happens . . . I would love to explain what it's like to be in the middle of a hundred people, all knowing and playing their part from the beginning to the end. But it's more than that, it's the sound that surrounds you that is phenomenal, and when that sound becomes magic, it cannot be described in words. I am so thankful I decided to do what I have done.

240

On Hearing a Symphony of Beethoven

Sweet sounds, oh, beautiful music, do not cease!
Reject me not into the world again.
With you alone is excellence and peace,
Mankind made plausible, his purpose plain.
Enchanted in your air benign and shrewd,
With limbs a-sprawl and empty faces pale,
The spiteful and the stingy and the rude
Sleep like the scullions in the fairy-tale.
This moment is the best the world can give:
The tranquil blossom on the tortured stem.
Reject me not, sweet sounds! oh, let me live,
Till Doom espy my towers and scatter them.
A city spell-bound under the aging sun,
Music my rampart, and my only one.

—*Edna St. Vincent Millay*